Fireside Reader

THE COUNSEL

Fireside Reader

20th Anniversary Selection
FROM THE PAGES OF COUNSEL MAGAZINE

GOSPEL FOLIO PRESS
304 Killaly Street West, Port Colborne, ON L3K 6A6
Available in the UK from JOHN RITCHIE LTD.
40 Beansburn, Kilmarnock, Scotland

All chapters were previously published as articles in *Counsel* magazine.

Published by Gospel Folio Press
304 Killaly Street West
Port Colborne, ON L3K 6A6
Web store: www.gospelfolio.com
Order phone line in North America: 1-800-952-2382

ISBN 1-882701-84-4

Printed in The United States of America

TABLE OF CONTENTS

COMPILER'S FOREWORD

ight men gathered in Tillsonburg, Ontario on June 28, 1980. They had just attended the funeral in Galt of a beloved brother in the Lord, Robert McClurkin, the founding editor of *Counsel* magazine. Present at that meeting were eight men: Neil Dougal (MA), John Elliott (MO), George Heidman (NB), Stuart Heinrich (MO), Leonard Lindsted (KS), J. Boyd Nicholson (ON), and Milo Vandekrol (IA). They were there to discuss the future ministry of the magazine. At that time it was determined, before the Lord, that the work should carry on, and Boyd Nicholson was asked to take the helm as editor.

For the next twenty years, *Counsel* became a welcome visitor in the homes of thousands of believers worldwide. There were many other Christian magazines with better paper, more pictures, and trend-setting typography. But it was the recurring testimonial of many that there was not a more Christ-exalting magazine to be found anywhere.

How could one magazine—in a day of such super-specialization—meet the heart needs of so many? It was read by sage elders and by college students, by homemakers and by prison inmates. Evangelists and Bible teachers in Zambia, India, Malaysia, and many Eastern European countries (where few or no Bible commentaries exist) pored over its pages, and then preached the truths it contained. Some copies of the magazine passed from hand to hand in a village, or through a prison cell block until they were tattered with use. Again we ask: How could one publication reach so many lives like that?

The Lord Jesus Himself declared: *"And I, if I be lifted up from the earth, will draw all men unto Me"* (Jn. 12:32). If the Lord Jesus Christ, repository of every spiritual blessing, is lifted up, there is not one child of God who cannot find exactly what he or she needs. This is the secret of *Counsel* magazine, and it was the secret of the editor's far-flung preaching ministry as well.

It had been the editor's desire to see a volume like this, whose contents would be selected from the magazines published during his tenure. But it was one project that his busy life did not permit. Now, following his passage to *"the land of far distances"* the present *Counsel* committee has decided to have published this "Fireside Reader" as a memorial to the diligent and devoted ministry of J. Boyd Nicholson to the readers of *Counsel* magazine.

It is to be noted that most of the Editor's writings are selected after 1993 since many of his editorials up to that date were already included in his much appreciated book, *The Watered Garden.*

The stated purpose of *Counsel* is to "give a variety of ministry by edification, exhortation, and comfort." It is now the heartfelt prayer of both the *Counsel* committee and of the Publishers that these selections will stir us up, build us up, and cause us to look up in devotion—and expectation—for our blessed Saviour and Lord.

J. B. NICHOLSON, JR.
November 2001

1. HEART PAIN

hen we were able to get a few days off duty, Harry, my navigator (a fellow-believer) and I would take the train to an Indian village north of Pune, where there was a mission for children. Some of these had been abandoned, some rescued from horrible fates. There they were lovingly cared for by a dedicated staff of missionaries and their helpers.

It wasn't only a welcome relief for us to get away, it was a delight to be with the children for a while. We got to know some of them in a special way.

One little fellow latched onto Harry and followed him like a puppy dog. In his little gray shirt, I thought he looked like a wee fellow in a kilt, so we called him MacGregor.

Then there was a beautiful little girl about 7 or 8 with those dark sparkling Indian eyes and long black tresses and a smile that would melt a stone. Her name sounded like it ended in Kukula, so I just called her "Cookie" for short.

We became good friends. Wherever I would be around the mission with the children, there she was, never far behind. Her mother, who worked at the mission, was a believer with a tragic story. A thief had broken into their home and killed Cookie's father as they lay in bed together. The widow and fatherless had been taken into the mission and lovingly cared for. There Cookie and her mother came to know the Lord.

Well, at last the day came when we had to move on. Our squadron was posted into Burma and we would have to say goodbye to our little friends. We made a last visit to see them and to tell them we were going away.

As Cookie and I walked around among the other children, I tried to get up the courage to tell my little friend that I would never see her again on earth.

At last I got down and told her, "Cookie, I have to go away now, and after a while, Lord willing, I will go back to my own country. I won't ever be able to come back and see you." My heart was aching as I looked at her. She looked a little puzzled, but didn't say a word, nor did she seem in any way upset. I was glad about that, and excused myself to go back to my room for a little rest.

I was sitting on the bed taking off my shoes when there was a quiet knock at the door. It was a screen door and I could see it was Cookie's mother. She knocked quietly again, so I rose and went to the door to ask her what she would like. Then I saw Cookie, hiding in the folds of her mother's sari. "May we come in, Sahib? Cookie says she has something to ask you."

"Of course," I replied, opening the door.

I went back and sat on the edge of the bed. Little Cookie came and stood beside me, patting my arm and saying, "My Sahib."

"What do you want to ask me, Cookie?" I asked. Then she spoke in her own language, which of course I could not understand. Turning to her mother I asked, "What is she saying?"

"She wants to go with you to your country."

"Oh, Cookie, I'm sorry," I said, "I can't take you away. I'm not married and have no home of my own. Anyway, you wouldn't like it there. It rains a lot and in the winter it is dark a long time and gets very cold, and your Mom would miss her little girl too much."

I don't think I will ever erase that look from my memory. She lifted those dark eyes, brimming with tears and looked at me. Then without another word she turned and went out the door. Nor can I forget the pain in my heart that day, a pain I had never felt before as I saw her little form go through the door and out of my life.

But I was giving her up to those who loved her, to those who would care for her every need, who would laugh with her and enjoy life together and protect her.

Right then as I felt that pain I thought, Whatever must it have meant to God the Father to yield up His only Son? Not into the arms of waiting lovers, but to those who would mock and insult Him, who would revile Him and spit in His face. Instead of the kiss and the crown, the Father saw them give Him the thorn, the spittle, the lash, and the nail to fasten Him to the only throne men ever gave Him.

O be silent, my soul! The Father has drawn the shroud of darkness around that sight. No mortal must see that visage now, marred more than any man. *"The Lord is in His holy temple: let all the earth keep silence before Him."* He draws the sword from its flaming scabbard—the sword that I deserve—to plunge it into the sinless yet sin-bearing soul of the Good Shepherd, the Scapegoat, the Sacrifice.

We sinners, though redeemed, will never know the unfathomable sorrows of God—Father, Son and Holy Spirit. But because of this we shall never know the ultimate sorrow of separation from God.

We wonder, we adore, and we worship.

—*J. Boyd Nicholson, Editorial, March-April 1999, p. 3*

2. THE BLESSING OF JABEZ

 any a Christian spends his days in grief and defeat because he has taken no steps to drive out the enemy from his rightful possession. We need to pray as did Jabez, *"Bless me indeed."*

Jabez was blessed in Judah, his father. It was written for him in the Word of God. Jabez could put his finger on the very words of the blessing! He could even put his own name in the verse as if it read thus, *"This is the blessing of [Jabez]: and he said: Hear, Lord, the voice of [Jabez] and bring him unto his people: let his hands be sufficient for him: and be Thou an help to him from his enemies"* (Deut. 33:7). Thus Jabez in Judah was blessed.

BLESSED INDEED

Jabez wanted to be blessed *indeed.* What did it avail to have the words of his blessing in the Book of God while the Canaanite enemy held the valleys of Judah's inheritance? What blessing was it when he had to stay on the grazing hills and see the entrenched Canaanite in his fruitful valleys (Jud. 1:19)? Jabez longed to possess his possessions.

The title-deeds of Judah were given in Joshua 15. Here the valleys as well as the hills were given to Judah and his children. There was the valley of Achor (Josh. 15:7), the valley of the giants (Josh. 15:8) and the valley with the fourteen cities (Josh. 15:33-36). What a loss to Judah—and Jabez—to see the valleys occupied by the Canaanites!

So Jabez prayed to the God of Israel who had given the whole land to Abraham's seed (Gen. 15:18). This is his prayer: *"Oh, that Thou wouldest bless me indeed, and enlarge my coast; and that Thine hand might be with me: and that Thou wouldest keep me from evil, that it may not grieve me"* (1 Chron. 4:10).

Jabez wanted his coast enlarged, not to include what was his brethren's, but to include what was his own and was still held by the enemy. Jabez wanted those valleys that were covered with corn, that he might shout for joy and sing (Ps. 65:13). Jabez wanted his valleys that grew grapes like those of Eshcol. Jabez wanted the valleys where grew the roses and the lilies that spoke of Him who is *"the Rose of Sharon and the Lily of the valleys"* (Song of Sol. 2:1). Jabez prayed for his coast to be *enlarged.*

HE DID SOMETHING ABOUT IT

Jabez did not expect God to send an angel from heaven to drive out the Canaanite. Neither did he look for God to use his brethren to enlarge his coast. Jabez expected God to use *him,* for it was part of the blessing that *"his hands [shall] be sufficient for him."*

So Jabez prayed that *"Thine hand might be with me."* Jabez did not intend to pray and just sit still. As far as he was able, this son of Judah was ready to bring his prayer to pass. He girded on his armor to enter his valleys with God. Those valleys would be his when he set his feet upon them (Josh. 1:3). Jabez acted to bring his prayers to pass.

I heard of a little girl who told her mother about her brother who had made cruel traps to catch God's little sparrows. She said, "I have prayed to God that he won't catch one, and I don't believe he will." "How can you be sure?" asked her mother. "Well, I kicked the old traps all to pieces." She did what she could to make her prayer effectual.

Jabez did the same. He looked at the record of his blessing and then looked to God and prayed a prayer of faith. Then he buckled on his sword and counted on God to be with him. This is how God granted, and how Jabez obtained, the *"blessing indeed"* that he desired.

Like Jabez, we are blessed through the Prince of the house of Judah. God *"hath blessed us with all spiritual blessings in heavenly places in Christ"* (Eph.1:3). But if we would be blessed *indeed* we need to *"put on the whole armor of God"* (Eph. 6:11). Like the enjoyment Jabez obtained from the fruit of the valleys, we shall enjoy the fruit of the Spirit in our lives only as we go in by faith and possess our possessions.

The enemy will dispute every foot of progress. We need to be *"praying always with all prayer and supplication in the Spirit...watching thereunto with all perseverance and supplication for all saints"* (Eph. 6:18).

THE NEED FOR SOUL EXERCISE

The prayer of Jabez is very short. It can be prayed in fifteen seconds. But there was much exercise of soul going before it. When the whole soul of Jabez was stirred because of the presence of the Canaanite in the inheritance of the Lord of hosts, then he *"called on the God of Israel."* With his prayer went the needed action, and this man, who was more honorable than his brethren, gained that victory that made him in a real way the possessor of his possessions.

May we not rest content with only being blessed in the purposes of God—may we go on to be *"blessed indeed."* If our lives are barren of the evidences of God's Spirit, let us do something about it! If the valleys do not ring with shouting and song, let us *"in the power of His might"* drive the giants out!

The Valley of Achor was in Judah's possessions. "Achor" means "trouble." Israel is to sing there in a day to come (Hos. 2:15). Many of our greatest blessings come through the valley of trouble. Let us not allow the Canaanite to possess our valley of Achor.

We should know that *"all things work together for good to them that love God"* (Rom. 8:28). In the end, Job's "valley of Achor" was covered with corn and song. The darkest hours of our lives can *"work for us a far more exceeding and eternal weight of glory"* (2 Cor. 4:17). Many a Christian spends his days in grief and defeat because he has taken no steps to drive out the enemy from his rightful possessions. We need to pray the prayer of Jabez of old to be *"blessed indeed."*

—Leonard Sheldrake, September-October 1998, pp, 12-13

3. THE GLORY OF THE EMPTY TOMB

e were standing on the mezzanine of the Veteran's Hospital in Paris, France. Beneath us on the ground level, and filling our gaze, was a great marble sarcophagus. Surrounded by magnificent frescoes and black marble pillars, each decorated with gold-encrusted capitals, it proclaimed in solemn dignity and singular immensity a single word, carved in the figured roseate stone, "NAPOLEON." It was the final repository of the mortal remains of the great French emperor.

Our lady guide drew herself to her full height and, almost snapping to attention, with a wave of the hand and with deep national pride and obvious emotion, she said, "Ici la gloire du France." Here is the glory of France.

The glory was not the magnificent casket, the frescoes or the pillars—the palace at Versailles has all that—but the mortal dust and crumbling bones of an emperor long gone and the memories imprisoned there.

About ten days later, while staying at a hotel on the Mount of Olives, I rose early and slipped out before the group had stirred. I made my way to another tomb. I wanted to be alone there for a while in the old garden that had been laid out at the base of Gordon's Calvary. For there is the tomb reputed to be the place where the body of the Lord Jesus lay.

After sitting quietly awhile, I stepped inside the tomb. As I looked around the stone floor and walls, the emptiness of the place impressed itself upon me and the very stone seemed to be reverberating with the words of the shining messengers long ago, *"He is not here, but is risen."* With deep feeling, I could not restrain myself from speaking out in that empty tomb, "Here is the glory of Christ!" No mouldering bones, no handful of ancient dust, no occupied casket—He is not here! We sing with joy:

Death cannot keep his prey, Jesus, my Saviour,
He tore the bars away, Jesus, my Lord.

15

Up from the grave He arose,
With a mighty triumph o'er His foes;
He arose the Victor from the dark domain,
And He lives forever with His saints to reign.
He arose! He arose!
Hallelujah! Christ arose! (Robert Lowry)

The resurrection of the Lord Jesus Christ is the keystone of the Christian faith and the heart of the Christian message. It was the first declaration of the disciples after the cross, *"The Lord is risen indeed."* It was the theme of Peter's message on the birthday of the Church, *"Jesus of Nazareth whom God hath raised up, having loosed the pains of death..."* Matthias, who replaced Judas in the apostolic ministry, was *"ordained to be a witness...of the resurrection."*

This is the basis of our faith. Without this great foundation, everything else is an eternal futility. Paul affirms in 1 Corinthians 15, *"If Christ be not risen..."* then preaching is vain; witnessing is false; believing is groundless; forgiveness is meaningless; and trusting loved ones have perished in some hopeless oblivion. *"But,"*—O thank God for that—*"now is Christ risen from the dead."*

It is also the basis of our hope. This mighty act was promised in the Psalms: *"Thou wilt not leave My soul in sheol, neither wilt Thou allow Thine Holy One to see corruption"* (Ps. 16:10, JND). It was pictured in the Scriptures: Isaac returning from the place of death portrays the resurrection of the Son in relation to the Father and His love. Aaron's rod that budded pictures the resurrection of the Stem, in relation to the Spirit and His fruit. Jonah delivered from the deep, pictures the resurrection of the Servant in relation to the Son and His suffering.

This mighty act was performed by the Triune God. It was the work of the Father of glory (Eph. 1:17-20). It was the work of the Spirit of grace (Rom. 8:9-11). Most wondrously it was also the work of the Son of God Himself (Jn. 2:19-22). He said of His body, *"I will raise it up again."* Talk about a miracle! A dead Man raising His own body to life! It is the supreme miracle, more magnificent than the creation of worlds.

It is the basis of our love. This is implicit in three words: *"preaching"* (1 Cor. 15:14)—this suggests our love to the saints in preaching the Word; *"witnesses"* but not false, suggesting our love to the lost; and *"testified"* suggests our love for the Lord Himself, as we witness "concerning God" in a hostile world.

This mighty truth should govern our present behavior (Rom. 6:4). It should inspire our constant anticipation (1 Cor. 15:22-23), and it should intensify our daily witness to all who are *"dead in trespasses and sins"* (Eph. 2:1).

—J. Boyd Nicholson, Editorial, March-April 1994, p. 3

4. JEREMIAH, THE WEEPING PROPHET

J t is not to the credit of the word makers that they have fashioned a dismal noun from the name of Israel's great prophet. The dictionary defines a "jeremiad" as "a doleful story." As a matter of fact, Jeremiah merely told the unpleasant truth about sin and its consequences and if his message had been believed, he would have been famous as the saviour of his country.

The ministry of this prophet is like that of a lighthouse built on a dangerous coast. It is equipped with dependable visual and audible warning devices, yet piled beneath it and all along the shore is the wreckage of ships, which, passing in the night, would not regard the signal beam nor heed the warning sound.

JEREMIAH MIGHT BE SEEN AS UNSUCCESSFUL

One of the disturbing habits of our day is to praise the successful and blame the unsuccessful—especially when the latter has no thrilling story to tell. Even though calloused knees and well-worn hands bear witness to unrelenting toil, there is a suspicion that somehow or other this seemingly unsuccessful servant has been secretly unfaithful, or his friends all have failed in their prayer responsibility. Both are common failings, but for one man to charge another with them is impertinence. Who are we to judge another's servant?

The words, *"He did not many mighty works there because of their unbelief"* (Mt. 13:58) ought to cheer workers in places of difficult service. This is not to excuse those who continue to plow the rock and sow among thorns while fields of white harvest wait for even a few laborers. Happily, we are not the lords of the harvest charged to send our subjects where we think they should be.

The days of Jeremiah were strangely like our own, marked by change and crisis and disorder; days when the foundations were destroyed and the righteous knew not what to do. Those of us who can look back on the past as if they were the pages of an aging book, marvel at their amazing contents and thrill in expectation of what the remaining pages will yet reveal. How great an honor and responsibility it is to have come to the kingdom for such a time as this!

JEREMIAH WAS PREORDAINED FOR HIS HIGH CALLING

Before his birth as a priest he was chosen to be a prophet, not only to Israel but to the nations. He had no doubt about his mission. His eyes opened to see reality from the divine point of view. With the touch of the hand of God lingering on his lips, he went where he was sent and did what he was told. How he anticipates Paul in this: *"...it pleased God who separated me from my mother's womb and called me by His grace, to reveal His Son in me that I might preach Him among the nations"* (Gal. 1:15–16). *"Before thy birth, I sanctified thee and ordained thee, a prophet unto the nations"* (Jer. 1:5, lit).

While we may not be able to fully grasp all the implications of the sovereignty of God and the free will of man, we ought to be able to assure our souls that even we who are numbered among the justified were foreknown and predestinated to be conformed to the image of the Son of God. This is the eminent source of confidence. The sovereign, distinguishing, inexplicable grace of God has moved and we are persuaded that nothing shall be able to separate us from His love.

Later, when overwhelmed by discouragement, Jeremiah cursed his day and wished he had never been born. But that was a passing experience which he has shared with many of us. To have known something of the depths of our own need and that of the lost world around us and to have known anything of the fellowship of the sufferings of Calvary is to have been near to the spirit of Jeremiah in his dark hour. It is such fearful storms which are hushed into calm by a commanding word from the mouth of the Lord.

JEREMIAH WAS A MAN WHO COULD PLEAD WITH MEN

His impassioned appeals are the stuff of abiding literature, but more, they are the expressions of a love that would not let his people go until he had spent all. In graphic Isaian language, he shows them their sin. They forsake the fountain of living waters and hew

19

out mere cisterns which break and never hold water. He sees them as a noble vine, once rich with promise of vintage, but now strangely changed into a degenerate plant. The lion of Judah has become the wild ass of the wilderness. The maid remembers her ornaments and the bride her attire, but the people of God have forgotten their Maker. He sees the birds on their migrations holding true to instinct. So different are they from Israel—lustful children, unnatural in their sin.

"When thou art spoiled, what wilt thou do?" he asks. *"How wilt thou do in the swelling of Jordan? What wilt thou say when He shall punish thee? What will ye do in the end thereof?"* Well they remembered his words when the harps of their minstrels hung silent and despairingly on the willows of Babylon. Mocking foreign tongues pleaded in vain for one of the songs of Zion.

JEREMIAH WAS A MAN OF PRAYER

His persistent pleading with men was the reaction of his prayer life. No mortal intercessor ever lived who was so bold in prayer. He cried, clinging to heaven by the hems. He used language which might well have earned rebuke. Instead it obtained promises.

We need not copy all his phraseology since the Son of God has come, revealing the Father, to whom childlike words are due. But not all the prophet's prayers were so violently expressed. If he cried, *"Wilt Thou be unto me as a deceitful brook; as waters that fail?"* he also identified himself with the national sin and humbly besought the Lord,

> *Do Thou it for Thy name's sake: for our backslidings are many; we have sinned against Thee. O the hope of Israel, the Saviour thereof in time of trouble, why shouldest Thou be as a stranger in the land, and as a wayfaring man that turneth aside to tarry for a night?* (Jer. 14:7-8).

In him the strength of the prophet combined with the tenderness of the priest. He was the prophet who stood for God before men and the priest who stood for men before God. The exercise of such a dual ministry meant and still means little exterior quietness, but it demands that most intense interior quietness, the peace of God.

JEREMIAH WAS A MAN WITH AN INFLEXIBLE PURPOSE

He had been entrusted with his work and would do it; he could do no other. False prophets might taunt him; kings might imprison him; princes might threaten his life; famine might waste him, but he held to his course, enduring the long-drawn horrors of the siege and meeting the conquerors calmly, for he knew them to be the messengers of God.

JEREMIAH WAS A MAN WHO HAS LEFT US A SECRET

He has left us the secret of his victory in the midst of defeat. *"The Lord God hath given me knowledge and I know...."* It is the testimony of a man in possession of an experience which cannot be gainsaid. Much is still hidden from his view, but what he has seen suffices until the full splendor of the beatific vision is revealed. Since he knew that the thoughts of God toward him were thoughts of peace and not of evil, he was at all times the master of his circumstances. Although the city of David and the temple of Solomon were in ruins, he was the man with the true heart, persuaded that the Judge of all the earth would do only right. If he had his due, our dictionaries would be altered and his name would be a synonym for that high courage which out of weakness is made strong.

Was Jeremiah, after all, an unsuccessful servant? How was it that when Nebuchadnezzar took some of the royal seed to Babylon, four young men brought up in the corruption of the Judean court were found in the hour of trial to be made of stuff worthy of Abraham and David? They were more than conquerors for they challenged the power of their conquerors and won. We shall think that they had read Jeremiah's burned and re-written words (see Dan. 9:2), seen his holy living, and heard his burning pleas to the salvation of their souls— and Nebuchadnezzar's.

—A. C. Rose, July-August 1999, pp. 4-5

5. God's Bag Lady

he was well up in her eighties when I first met her. She lived in an upstairs apartment in a pleasant seacoast town in the west of Scotland. At least that is where she spent her latter years. The rest of her days had been spent in Africa as a missionary. Now Maggie lived alone—she would be quick to remind you she was never "alone," for the Lord was with her—and day by day as weather and strength permitted, she stuffed her old, oversize handbag with gospel papers and made her way to the sea front where people walked. There she continued her lifework of seeking the lost for the Master.

When I asked her what God had used that so affected her, that she yielded herself to the Lord and to a service that took her to Africa for a lifetime, she told me the following incident.

When as a young Christian, about 17, she felt that the Lord was calling her to some special service for Him somewhere. About that time, the renowned Dr. F. B. Meyer came to Glasgow to speak. She thought, such a man of God might have a word from the Lord for her, so she went to the city to hear him. He was then up in his eighties and rather weak, so that he had to sit while he spoke.

He recounted a life-changing incident in his experience when he was 60 years of age. Already a respected servant of God, he was fully occupied in preaching and writing. He began to labor under sheer exhaustion. Lord Strathclyde, a shipping magnate, heard about Dr. Meyer's need and invited him to spend some time for rest at his Scottish estate.

One day as the great preacher was walking in the quiet and peaceful grounds belonging to this Christian gentleman and enjoying the solitude, along the path came Lord Strathclyde himself. Dr. Meyer expressed his deep appreciation for this wonderful time of healing in such a beautiful spot. "Well," said the gentleman, "I haven't shown you my treasure yet. Follow me." Wondering what riches he was about to see, Dr. Meyer followed until he was led to a clearing in the trees. There before his eyes was an African-style hut. Lord

Strathclyde explained the reason for this unusual structure on his estate.

He had been privileged to attend the burial service of the great David Livingstone at Westminster Abbey. The African Christians had removed the heart of this missionary explorer and buried it in Africa, then brought his embalmed body to Britain for the burial. Those Africans were invited by Lord Strathclyde to enjoy a time of rest, as Dr. Meyer had been, before they would return to Africa.

These beloved servants of the Lord from the far-off land were most appreciative of such noble kindness and approached Lord Strathclyde one day to tell him that they wanted to give him something, but seeing his castle and obvious great wealth, did not know what they could ever impart to him.

There was one thing, he said. Would they build an exact replica of the African house where they had found the body of the great missionary, bowed over the bed, as he had been in prayer?

With native expertise, they cut down the trees, and with mud and straw completed the task, even making the furniture as it had been. Here was the house! They stepped inside.

Lord Strathclyde withdrew and left Dr. Meyer alone with his thoughts. As he looked around, he was suddenly overwhelmed with the immensity of the man, Dr. Livingstone, and the greatness of his work for God and for his beloved Africans. He threw himself down across the bed and cried out to God, "O God! Forgive me. I have only been halfhearted; take my will and make it Thine, and wherever I am out of joint with Thee, put me into joint, and as a token Thou has heard my cry, give me some special work to do."

Now the aged Dr. Meyer reported to his audience that God had given him his greatest work to do at home and for missionary work in Africa from that time, after he was 60 years of age.

Young Maggie had listened breathlessly to the story. Hurrying home, she threw herself on her knees across her bed and cried out to God the very same prayer of the great preacher. Eventually God led her to that same land and there she spent her life in the service of her Lord and Master.

As Maggie finished her story, she reached for her old Bible and opened the fly leaf. There I read in her own handwriting that prayer and the date she first prayed it. We read it over in silence. She closed the Book, "Every year from then till now, on that date I have prayed that prayer, lest even in my old age I should be out of joint with God's will—and d'ye know? He keeps on giving me work to do for Him."

Humbled, we rose to leave. Maggie turned to face us, took our hands in her old hands, and said, "Now, let us worship God!"

—J. Boyd Nicholson, Editorial, September-October 1994, p. 3

6. Bitter Herbs and the Blessed Hope

 et no man think the believer's sighs are the language of unbelief or his tears the expression of unconsoled sorrow. Let no presumptuous hand remove the bitter herbs from the paschal feast. It is a great forgiveness which God bestows, which Jesus purchased, which the Spirit seals, and we know it to be real. Yet as we feel God's forgiveness great, we cannot always forget our sins. They are blotted out, they are judged, they are crucified; we hate them, we fight against them; but there they are.

Our old man, with all its members, though crucified (Rom. 6:6) is still to be put off (Eph. 4:22). Grace has not annihilated it. Although grace enables us to reckon our old man crucified and calls us to mortify our members which are on earth (Col. 3:5), how can we help remembering what we were, and what we did, when sin, although no longer reigning within us, is still present with us; when the flesh still—daily and always—is in mortal enmity against the Spirit? Poor believer! Wretched man! Chief of sinners! God will comfort you. How often do you cry:

> *Say this word of love again,*
> *Christ receiveth sinful men!*

And how often does your soul respond,

> *Chief of sinners though I be,*
> *Christ is all in all to me!* (William McComb)

Believe and rejoice in the Lord. *"Worthy is the Lamb."* By faith behold the beauty of the Lord and sing:

> *Your many sins are all forgiven;*
> *Oh, hear the voice of Jesus!*
> *Go on your way in peace to heaven*
> *And wear a crown with Jesus.* (William Hunter)

The soul mourns over its sins and the pettiness of its good works. We feel grace wins only meager triumphs and wonder why sin is not exterminated. We are disappointed that the heavenly Gardener does not remove the bitter root altogether.

There are times when it is imagined that He has done so. A subtle and sweet calm, an unusual energy as of the Spirit, a happy freedom from the attacks of old sins and habits, seem for a while to descend on the soul; we feel ourselves pure, beautified, no longer in the wilderness, always victorious. Alas! it may well be the enemy appearing as an angel of light to put us off guard. The Lord Jesus Christ, the Crucified, Physician of the sick, Healer of the brokenhearted, Saviour of sinners, is not necessarily the root of such an experience. Such sweetness does not always come from the cleft of the Rock.

God's thoughts are not our thoughts; His ways are not our ways. We discover this continually. Not merely when we are first brought to a knowledge of salvation, and we see with rejoicing surprise the marvellous methods of free grace, but ever afterwards we learn that the ways of God are different from our wisdom and the expectation of our hearts.

How natural is the thought and desire of the soul that has begun to love Christ, that its progress may now be always continuous and rapid! How natural even the thought, that in some moment of faith and ardent soul-surrender, there will here be given from above a complete and final victory over the love of sin and the world! Yet how different is the experience of the embattled Christian! Is it not true of all, what an old saint describes as his personal history?

I asked the Lord that I might grow
In faith and love, and every grace;
Might more of His salvation know,
And seek more earnestly His face.

'Twas He who taught me thus to pray,
And He, I trust, has answered prayer;
But it has been in such a way
As almost drove me to despair.

I hoped that in some favored hour,
At once He'd answer my request,
And by His love's constraining power
Subdue my sins, and give me rest.

Instead of this, He made me feel
The hidden evils of my heart;
And let the angry powers of hell
Assault my soul in every part.

Yea, more; with His own hand He seemed
Intent to aggravate my woe;
Crossed all the fair designs I schemed,
Blasted my gourds; and laid me low.

"Lord, why is this?" I trembling cried;
"Wilt Thou pursue Thy worm to death?"
"'Tis in this way," the Lord replied,
"I answer prayers for grace and faith."

"These inward trials I employ,
From self and pride to set thee free;
And break thy schemes of earthly joy,
That thou mayst seek thine all in Me." (John Newton)

The heavenly wisdom explains that God has commanded us to *"fight the good fight of faith"* as long as we are on earth; the *"city of palm trees"* is beyond. Vision and unsullied joy await us in the heavenly Jerusalem. Our rest is in God even now; but it is not the rest of glory. The old man is not annihilated in us, or there would be no conflict.

Do we wish to be pure and faultless so that we would give the glory to God? If suddenly our sin was removed, would we ascribe it to God, and to God alone? Though we may say so with our lips, would our secret thoughts be, "I have done this"? Would not the enemy at least whisper into our hearts? Have we not at times experienced how a smooth and outwardly flawless life can conceal a disease more dangerous and loathsome—the sin of hard, self-contained and self-satisfied Pharisaism, which needs no Saviour and has no tears of joy, of gratitude, nor shame to shed?

We cannot be too earnest, too diligent, too watchful. We cannot possibly aim too high. We cannot have too much faith and hope in the power of the Lord Jesus. It is an essential feature in every Christian that there be a longing after holiness.

The following extract is from the diary of Philip M. Hahn (Feb. 8, 1786):

During my private prayer I remembered my impatient speech today, and this brought before me my sins in so clear a light, and with a deep feeling of sorrow and abhorrence. It showed me so clearly the necessity of an atonement, and the greatness of God's mercy, and that we live entirely by the grace of God, and are unworthy. I thought within myself, How instructive are our failures! For I know from experience that when some considerable time has passed without open failure, I become proud, unmerciful, self-complacent, censorious of others. God delights only in a childlike, humble heart. But this is by no means to encourage us in carelessness. It is to my shame that I have not the mind of Christ.

Are we children of God? Then the command follows naturally: *"Be ye holy, for I am holy."* Are we disciples of Christ? Then it is ours to learn of Him who was meek and lowly in heart. Are we His friends? Then it is for us to do whatsoever He commands us. Are we members of His Church, of the body of which He is the Head? Then it is for us to walk worthy of the vocation wherewith we are called and to remember that the Holy Spirit Himself dwells in us.

—Adolph Saphir, March-April 1997, pp. 6-7

t was a beautiful day in the fall of the year. The trees wore their golden regalia with dignity. But it was turning cold. Soon cumulo-nimbus giants were roiling in the distance, pushing their turrets ever higher till the altitude flattened their tops into the classic anvilhead of the massive stormcloud. It was too early for snow; the trees were still loaded with leaves and fruit. Too soon they came, a few flakes spinning down to tell us more were on the way. Sure enough, down they fell in large feathery deposits that quickly covered the ground and began to fill the trees.

Next morning we awoke to a dazzling display of winter's artistry. Then we saw it! A young maple tree on the front lawn that yesterday had looked so bright and straight in the sun. The trunk was split right to the ground. It had capitulated to the weight of the snow on the leaves. I had never seen such a thing before. That beautiful tree found the burden too heavy, and there it lay in an agony, torn apart.

I have often complained of the brevity of the glorious fall. So soon it is swept away into winter by the winds and heavy rains that tear the leaves from every branch. That day perhaps I understood a little more about the order of things. From a lesson of the broken tree I learned that the leaves must be stripped away, or else the tree would be broken under the weight of the snow.

The stark branches of the winter trees, colorless and bare, have as much beauty as a skeleton. But they can bear the weight of the snow, letting the storm whistle through their unlovely frame, bending and yielding to its blast. They wait for the return of spring. Then the sap will flow and life will burst forth in bud and blossom as the root draws from the earth sweetened by the winter snows.

Before the Lord Jesus went to the cross, He spent that memorable time alone with His disciples, mostly in the upper room. He showed them a living parable of His unfinished work *"out of this world"* on their behalf as He washed their feet, unfolded the Spirit to them, and interceded for them. He unfolded to them visions of glory beyond

Golgotha's gloom. How they needed that as they approached the sorrows of the next few days.

As He introduced them to the ministry of the Holy Spirit that would follow, He said, *"I have yet many things to say unto you, but ye cannot bear them now"* (Jn. 16:12). For the word *"bear"* He used an unusual verb in this connection. It speaks of the bearing of a burden. A full revelation of the cross and its mighty significance would be just too much for them at that time. Trembling and fearful and full of questions as they were then, they would have broken under it. They must pass through the winter's darkness first, when the sun refused to shine, and feel that they had lost everything precious to them. All their Treasure, their peace, and hope, would be nailed on a cross and torn from them. They themselves would learn something of the blasting storm in their own lives.

As Jacob discovered after the night of wrestling (Gen. 32:31), their sun would shine again. The Lord would arise and hope would spring up anew. Life would surge into their barren souls again. Then, by the Spirit's power, there would be fruit and flower, joy and rejoicing as they would learn that their beloved Lord was dwelling in their hearts by faith. They would reach out to apprehend the vastness of the love of Christ, and within be *"filled with all the fullness of God."*

God will never pour an ocean of blessing into an unprepared heart. He will always develop the vessel to contain the suited blessing. Otherwise the blessing would be a burden too heavy to bear.

Dear puzzled believer, follower of Christ, always seeking God's highest gifts and noblest benefits. You have prayed great prayers, sought mighty treasures from His Word. Instead has come the blast of winter winds, stripping you of your beauty and leaving the soul stark in your sorrowing night. You cry an anguished "Why?" into the dark.

Faint not, beloved! God has heard your great prayers. The answer is on the way, but first you must be *"strengthened with might by His Spirit in the inner man"* to bear the freight of blessings which you have sought. The stripping is the beginning of blessing!

Oft we shrink from the pruning and purging,
Forgetting the Husbandman knows

That the deeper the cutting and paring,
The richer the cluster that grows. (Anonymous)

You may not look as beautiful as once you were. You may no longer be praised in the sunlight as others seem to be. But God's hand has been on you; His storms have prepared you; He has stripped away your own glory; the deadwood is broken off. Soon the mighty sap of the Spirit's power will flow, and God will keep His promise. Thus you may glorify Him in your body and in your spirit, and many will bless the Lord that through your sorrows He has prepared you to be such a channel of His blessing.

—*J. Boyd Nicholson, Editorial, July-August 1990, p. 3*

8. LORD CALEB OF HEBRON

 aleb stands out as one of the spiritual giants of Old
Testament history, and while he is not mentioned in
Hebrews 11, we catch fleeting glimpses of his life in
the list of faith's exploits at the end of the chapter.

Who through faith subdued kingdoms, wrought righteousness, obtained
promises...escaped the edge of the sword, out of weakness were made strong,
waxed valiant in fight, turned to flight the armies of the aliens (Heb. 11:33-34).

"Obtained promises" are words which certainly bring Caleb to mind
and turn our thoughts to an historic scene in Joshua 14.

The place is Gilgal, and the central figures Caleb and Joshua, both
now advanced in years. The Israelites have already crossed Jordan,
invaded Canaan, routed enemy armies and shattered their alliances.
Though strong pockets of resistance still remain, the time has come
for Joshua to divide the land by lot among the tribes. As the tribal
heads gather, wondering where their various territories will lie,
Caleb arrives with a delegation from Judah, but he already knows
his inheritance and is determined to get it.

His case was simple, his logic clear. Had not his portion in
Canaan been already settled by divine decree? Had not God
promised, indeed sworn, that Hebron would be the possession of
Caleb and his descendants? Where God had thus spoken lots were
out of place. Caleb only needed Joshua, formally and publicly, to
declare Hebron his, so that he might proceed at once against the
giant brood that had squatted there so long.

This earnest appeal found a ready response in the heart of Joshua,
who endorsed Caleb's claim to Hebron—not just the city but the sur-
rounding region as well. *"Hebron therefore became the inheritance*
of Caleb..." (Josh. 14:14).

The promise on which Caleb based his claim sprang from events
in Numbers 13 and 14, but Hebron had a unique place in the Bible
story centuries before. We first meet the name in connection with
the life of Abraham when he *"moved his tent and came and dwelt by*

the oaks of Mamre, which are in Hebron, and built there an altar unto the Lord" (Gen. 13:18 NASB).

Just before this, he had received a potentially substantial promise from the Lord: *"All the land which thou seest, to thee will I give it and to thy seed for ever."* When we remember that, at some 3,000 feet above the Mediterranean, Hebron was the highest city in southern Canaan, we may well wonder if Abraham had sought a vantage point from which to view his promised possessions.

At the same time, Abraham had his eyes and heart set on a heavenly country (Heb. 11:16), and soon Hebron had *"an altar unto the Lord."* From the sight and smell of the sacrificial smoke drifting heavenward, the Canaanites—with their earth-bound gods—might quickly learn that the newcomer in their midst had links with the world above, and that, living in Canaan, his hopes were in heaven. How appropriate, then, that Abraham's new location among the Judean hills should bear the name Hebron which means firstly "union" and then "communion" or "fellowship."

Here Abraham *"dwelt"* for most of his remaining years, making it his main center of activity until his death. Here, too, he was buried; and later Isaac also. Then Jacob, on his death-bed in Egypt, gave instructions that he should be buried with them—heirs together of the same promise, in death as in life.

Each of the three patriarchs had received a double promise from the Lord: their seed would be a mighty nation, and Canaan would be their national home (Gen. 13:15-16; 26:3-4; 28:13-14). So when God linked His name with theirs at the call of Moses (Ex. 3:6), He showed His abiding commitment to His honored servants lying in distant Hebron.

This throws a flood of light on the account in Numbers 13 of the twelve spies sent by Moses to reconnoiter Canaan. *"They ascended...unto Hebron."* Of all the places they must have seen during their forty days in the land, the spotlight is on Hebron alone, with details of its great antiquity and warlike inhabitants. Hebron surely was sacred ground for any Israelite, a trysting place for past memories and future hopes, both for the individual and the nation.

The spies' report likewise showed that the Hebron area (to which the Vale of Eshcol belonged) was mainly in mind. Above all else, however, their words revealed their own state of heart, and divided Caleb and Joshua sharply from the other ten. Such belief and unbelief simply cannot co-exist; they are poles apart. Heaven's God or Hebron's giants—that was the issue. The ten feared giants; the two feared God. Of Caleb the Lord declared that he had *"another spirit"* (Num. 14:24), a spirit of which the despairing ten had no knowledge. They, by their demoralizing words, had set the people against their leaders and against God, whereas Caleb and Joshua sought to rally the people around the Lord's standard to invade the land.

Caleb had *"another spirit"* when he first set eyes on Hebron. Here was the place where the Creator and the creature had met and communed, where the invisible God had found means of making Himself known to men, where the very foundations of his faith had been disclosed. How could a man ponder such things and not be profoundly moved? Caleb took Hebron to his heart that day, and in spirit told the giants to begone.

Caleb had *"another spirit"* too in Kadesh as he faced over half a million able-bodied men who were ready to stone anyone who told them the truth. He possessed that *"spirit of faith"* of which Paul spoke in 2 Corinthians 4:13, a spirit which causes a man to voice his beliefs and fearlessly declare all that is in his heart (Josh. 14:7). *"We are well able to overcome,"* insisted Caleb. *"The Lord is with us: fear them not."* But all was in vain; an epidemic of incredulity and hostility had swept through the camp and brought the nation under Jehovah's chastening rod.

Caleb had, and needed, *"another spirit"* for the next four decades as he trudged through the desert among a fractious people. But their murmurings could never drown the promises of God in Caleb's soul. The swirling sands might blind him to much around, but could never dim his vision of Hebron. He though about it by day, and dreamed about it by night. Hebron. HEBRON! How could he ever forget it?

Such was the man who stood before Joshua in Gilgal, wanting Hebron more than anywhere else on earth (Josh. 14:6-15). Though an octogenarian, he had retained the vigor of middle life and the winsome trust of a child. Where he seemed to obtrude himself into the picture, it was only to recall what the Lord had said and done.

Twice do we read here of Caleb's non-Israelitish background—he was a Kenezite whose clan had apparently been merged in Judah—but in the lineage of faith Abraham had few more worthy sons.

Like Jacob too, Caleb had laid hold on God and men, and refused to let go until he got the blessing. *"Give me this mountain, whereof the Lord spake."* And the giants? *"I shall be able to drive them out, as the Lord said."* Woe to any son of Anak who might have crossed the path of Caleb as he left Gilgal with Joshua's blessing.

Caleb went into action with the full assurance of God's promise, God's presence, and God's power. Elsewhere the Israelites engaged the enemy with the palsied arm of unbelief, but Caleb's arm was made strong by the hands of the mighty God of Jacob. So Caleb fought, giants fled, and Hebron fell. Soon his forces were hammering on the gates of Debir, about 13 miles away, with Caleb offering his daughter in marriage to the man who took it.

In other parts of the land strong enemy groups still remained, but Caleb flushed every vestige of them out of Hebron and soon the whole area *"had rest from war."* In a British context, Caleb's undoubted valor and signal victories could well have earned a peerage, and he could have come down to us in history as Lord Caleb of Hebron.

—W. P. W. McVey, November-December 1983, pp. 6-7

9. WORTH A THOUSAND WORDS

Beautiful! You should see her! Just like her dad! She takes after your side of the family! Her chin—her nose—her wee head—no, not much hair yet. We'll send you a picture as soon as we can." So went the conversation over the long-distance phone lines. We had just been informed of the latest addition to our family of another baby girl. After some conversation about weights and measures, we hung up. "If only we had a picture," we said, for the old adage is right, "A picture is worth a thousand words."

God Himself understands our limitations, especially when it comes to things divine and eternal that are not naturally discerned. So in grace He has revealed Himself in many graphic ways. He has declared His mighty power and supreme intelligence in the vastness of the universe. He has shown His wisdom in the wonders of nature. But all the revelations of God in the material universe must fade before the greatest of all, the revelation of Himself in His Son. This is a revelation of His matchless love.

As a Father, God is delighted to show forth the excellence and beauty of His beloved Son by many revelations in His Word, if by any means He might call forth our worship, love and praise.

In His Word, He utilizes every device of human language to present in countless word-pictures the wonders of the Lord Jesus. He uses statements of plain language; proclamations of predictive prophecy; types and shadows, parables and allegories, figures and emblems to show to us the *"mystery of godliness"*—God manifest in the flesh. God the Father plunders every realm of His universe to show these beautiful pictures of His dear Son.

From the wonders of space, God shows His excellent glories: the sun in the heavens pictures His beneficent and life-giving powers every day, shining upon the evil and the good. What a glorious pyrotechnic of the amazing grace of God! God's Son is seen in *"the bright and morning star"* as it rises before the daybreak and portrays to all the dependability and accuracy of God's promise and the certainty of the coming dawn. Light itself in all its radiant spectrum shows forth the glories of the Lord Jesus. The blue light of His heavenly effulgence, the green light of His abundant and eternal life, the red light, that shadowless hue of heaven, the light of the Lamb, diffuse together in the brilliance of uncreated beams of the One who is the Light of the world.

From the atmosphere, God draws forth still more radiant pictures of His beloved Son. The rainbow pictures His everlasting mercy and the morning dew His daily refreshing. The sparrow alone upon the housetop, the pelican in the place of judgment, and the owl seeing afar, all speak of Him.

The earth and its store join together to tell His worth. The mines of gold, of costly stones and precious silver, yield still more pictures of a Redeemer who is God, the altogether lovely One.

The waters are plumbed and drawn forth to portray the depth of His suffering, the resources of His refreshing, and the ministry of His life-giving powers as the well, the spring, the fountainhead.

The animal world must parade its glory to display the wonders of God's Son. The lion, the lamb, and the gentle deer, show forth His power, His meekness, gentleness, and His sensitivity.

Still there are more and more revelations of God in His beloved Son. In a plethora of delight, the Father shows the Son in the stones of architecture, the great Foundation stone of the Church, the Corner and the Cornice stone, where every angle meets and every line of perspective draws the eye to focus on His glory as the risen Head. The seeds of agriculture are used to tell us of One who went into the ground and died in view of a most plenteous harvest. The very ground itself yields a harvest of pictures of the Son of God. The apple tree, the vine, the root, the stem, the lily of the valley and the rose of Sharon all breathe His fragrance and bear fruit.

The armory trumpets His glory in the shield, the buckler, the sword and the battle bow, to assure us of His mighty resources for the conflict day by day.

Pigments of color; fragrances of ointment; tones of music, flashes of lightning and rolling of thunder: all portray some wonder of God's beloved Son. We stand amazed in the midst of God's gallery of glory. We gaze in breathless wonder at every picture of His beloved Son, and we bow at the call of the psalmist, *"He is thy Lord; and worship thou Him"* (Ps. 45:11).

Oh, yes! We did get a picture of our new wee baby. I carry it with me everywhere and delight to show it when I can. Should I not always be as ready to speak and show the wonders, the exquisite beauties and mighty works, of our glorious Lord and Saviour until that day when we shall be like Him, *"for we shall see Him as He is"*?

—*J. Boyd Nicholson, Editorial, May-June 1994, p. 3*

10. Fragrance for Christ

was tired, and sat down under the shadow of the great pines in a Swedish forest, glad to find such a cool retreat from the broiling sun. I had not been there long before I noticed a fragrant odor and wondered what it could be and where it came from.

No fragrant rose grew there, nor could the sun penetrate the shades of the forest to extract its perfume even if it had. I looked round, and found by my side a tiny flower about half the size of an ordinary daisy, nearly hidden from view by the moss. It was the little *Linéa blomma*.

Oh, how fragrant it was! Again and again I leaned over to more fully enjoy the perfume, and then I looked up and thanked God for that tiny flower—so insignificant, growing in a wild, almost untrodden forest, yet bringing cheer and refreshment to me.

I thought, why is it so obscure when it is a flower with such fragrance, and surely worthy of a place in the most stately grounds? I learned a lesson by it, and it spoke powerfully to my heart. I thought, if I cannot be a mighty pine in God's forest, I may be a tiny flower to send forth the fragrance of Jesus in this world of sadness.

There is a tendency in our hearts to desire to be or to do something great. We are not content, like the tiny *Linéa* flower, to send forth fragrance in obscurity.

I have often met the Lord's people despondent over the apparent uselessness of their lives. They cannot point to some great deed accomplished for the Lord. It has never been theirs to figure prominently in His service, nor have they the remembrance of having done anything worthy of record.

It is written, *"And seekest thou great things for thyself? Seek them not..."* (Jer. 45:5). Beloved fellow believer, let me tell you it is possible for you to be fragrant in this world. Keep close to Christ, walk in happy communion with Him; let your heart drink in His love and you will be fragrant to Him.

Could you conceive anything greater than that? No eye may see you but His; no ear may hear you but His; no heart appreciate your act or thought but His; but how precious—I can be fragrant to the Lord Jesus! Nothing surely is so delightful to Him as to have you and me walking with Him. If this is so, we shall also surely come in contact with some weary soul who needs refreshment. We can speak of Jesus, and in such a way that there will be Christlikeness about us.

Dear fellow believer, let us give up the disappointing business of self-occupation. As long as we are occupied with self, we are not occupied with Christ. True greatness is the measure in which the excellence of Christ flows forth from us.

"His name is as ointment poured forth." While down here, the Lord Jesus Christ was not great as men count greatness. His was a life of obscurity. He chose no place of prominence. When by force they would make Him king, He retired to a deserted place; when His brethren pressed Him to go up to the feast to do some great miracle and show Himself, He answered, *"My time is not yet come."* To do His Father's will was His one commanding business. He was that *"Root out of a dry ground"* who could say, *"All My springs are in Thee."*

What fragrance came forth from Him! *"All Thy garments smell of myrrh, and aloes, and cassia, out of the ivory palaces, whereby they have made thee glad"* (Ps. 45:8). All those who were far from God could smell the holy perfume and say, *"Never man spake like this man."* The heartless Pilate had to say, *"I find no fault in this man."* The centurion at the cross had to confess, *"Certainly this was a righteous man."* Others could but marvel at *"the gracious words that proceeded out of His mouth."*

None could come into His presence without smelling the fragrant odors of love, compassion, and tenderness. The wickedness of the human heart, which He met on every hand, disclosed His preciousness more and more. Let us then not be despondent over what we are and what we are not. Let our attention be more than ever directed to Him, so that as He fills our vision, everything else may vanish. As His sweetness fills the soul, so will His fragrance flow forth from us as the outcome of communion with Him.

May the Lord, then, so attach our hearts to Himself that, like the little *Linéa* flower sending forth its perfume in the untrodden forest, we may send forth by His Spirit and for His own pleasure something of His fragrance in this world and so be a reflection of the only perfect and fragrant One, our Lord Jesus Christ.

—J. H. Lewis, January-February 1991, p. 14

11. THE SEVEN CONSOLATIONS OF CHRIST

Jn John 14:1-27, beginning with the words *"Let not your heart be troubled"* and ending with the words *"Let not your heart be troubled, neither let it be afraid,"* the Saviour gives seven consolations for *"His own"* who are left in the world. They are words of greatest comfort to encourage and strengthen us until He comes to take us all home above.

CONSOLATION ONE:
Our reunion with Him in the Father's home (vv. 1-3)

The Lord reveals six facts about the home.

• *Its reality* (vv. 1-2). This is based upon our faith in God, in Christ, and in His Word.

• *Its locality* (v. 2). It is a definite *"place,"* in distance far beyond our comprehension, but where the Father dwells, where the Son is amidst holy angels, and where loved ones are now *"with Christ."*

• *Its felicity* (v. 1). No troubles there! Thus He can say to His own, *"Let not your heart be troubled."* It is a home of rest (Heb. 4:9), joy (Ps. 16:11), love (1 Cor. 13:13), and fellowship (Rev. 21:3; 22:3-5).

• *Its immensity* (v. 2). It is described as containing *"many mansions."* Multitudes will be there (Rev. 5:11; 7:9). The Father's house will be filled (Lk. 14: 23; Isa. 53:11).

• *Its permanency* (v. 2). The Greek word for *"mansions"* describes its abiding character; it is a place where we will eternally dwell. It is our permanent home (Heb. 11:10; 13:14).

• *Its imminency* (v. 3). The Lord has promised to come personally (1 Thess. 4:16) and suddenly (1 Cor. 15:52; Rev. 22:7; 12, 20) for His people. Our hearts cry, Perhaps today! Blessed consolation!

CONSOLATION TWO:
We know the way to the Father's home (vv. 4-11)

The way is *a Person*, One whom we have trusted. The way is *suf-*

ficient. Why? First, He is the truth, the full and perfect revelation of God His Father (Heb. 1:3; Col. 1:19). Second, He is the life, the personal embodiment of eternal life (1 Jn. 5:12). The way is *exclusive*. This is of great significance because He is the only way, not one of many ways (Jn. 10:9). To come to the Father one must have Christ. The absolute *perfection* of the way is revealed in verses 7-11, for the Father is fully revealed in and by the Son. We must understand that when we come to the Son, we come to the Father. Then with confidence we can say we know the way. Blessed consolation!

CONSOLATION THREE:
Though in heaven, our Lord still works on the earth (vv. 12-14)

His chosen vessel is the believer (v. 12). *The character of the works*: they are similar to His own (v. 12). His early disciples did them (Acts 3:6-8; 9:40; 11:13; 16:18; 20:12, etc.). Also they are greater works, for they are miracles of a spiritual kind (see Peter, Acts 2:41; Philip, Acts 8:5-12; Paul on all his missionary travels). Why greater works? *"Because I go to My Father"* (see Jn. 7:37-39; 16:7). The exaltation of Christ and the descent of the Spirit have produced these *"greater works."* Notice *how* the work is done (vv. 13-14)—through communication between Christ and the believer. By His Spirit and the Word, Christ communicates His will to the believer. Then by prayer to the Father, the believer communicates with Him. But the Lord Himself is the real worker; we are His instruments. He continues to work through us. *"Without Me, ye can do nothing!"* (Jn. 15:5). Blessed consolation!

CONSOLATION FOUR:
The promise of another Comforter (vv. 15-17)

This other Comforter is personal and divine, One who is like Myself, says the Lord. He is equal with the Father and the Son, though He is distinct from both. The condition of enjoying Him is found in verse 15: love for the Lord and our obedience to His Word. Two blessed facts are given to us here. First, His *permanent* presence: *"with you for ever"* (v. 16). Second, His *indwelling* presence: *"in you."* The Spirit of Truth is His name, come to reveal all truth to

His own. Can we ever lose Him? Never! Blessed consolation!

CONSOLATION FIVE:
The return of the glorified Christ (vv. 18-24)

It is *spiritual*, not His post-resurrection ministry, but a return in the Person of the Holy Spirit. It is *personal, "I will come to you"* (v. 18). Note also verses 21 and 23. During our Lord's sojourn on earth the Spirit was personally present with Him. So after His departure, Christ is personally present with us by the Spirit. By faith *"we see Jesus"* (Heb. 2:9). We participate in His risen life (v. 19b). We apprehend His greatness, His oneness with the Father; our oneness with Him; and His oneness with us (v. 20). He reveals Himself and His Father (vv. 21, 23). Are we enjoying this? It is a blessed consolation.

CONSOLATION SIX:
The mission of the Holy Spirit (vv. 25-26)

The Holy Spirit should be held in highest esteem. He is the saints' Comforter. He is the Father's Representative, sent by the Father. He is also the saints' Teacher: *"He shall teach you all things."* He is the saints' Remembrancer, bringing *"all things to your remembrance."* He is the Saviour's Expositor: in *"whatsoever I have said unto you."* Concerning more of His work, read John 15:26; 16:7-13. Without His ministry, Christ would never be revealed nor understood. We can depend on Him. Blessed consolation!

CONSOLATION SEVEN:
The Saviour's legacy of peace for all circumstances (v. 27)

It is the peace of contentment in all our circumstances. This peace the world can never learn, nor give us. Unrest and discontent prevail today. Only one Man has appeared on earth who never needed to search for peace! From the beginning of His life to the end He possessed it! He was never ruffled, never fretting over His external circumstances nor the privations He endured. The reproaches He encountered, the sufferings He bore, even the death that He died, never disturbed His peace. In the midst of it all He had *"perfect peace"* (Isa. 26:3). This same peace He has bequeathed to His own.

He gives it generously, sincerely, and permanently. This legacy the Saviour has given us to sustains us in the midst of our trials. It is not merely a peace that He can impart but a peace which He Himself possessed—*"My peace."* Is it ours today? Blessed consolation!

THE PURPOSE OF THESE SEVEN CONSOLATIONS:
"Let not your heart be troubled, neither let it be afraid."

Our blessed Lord unfolds these great consolations from His own loving heart to the hearts of His followers to strengthen them in view of His departure out of this world to the Father and to sustain His own until He comes back. Is there trouble? Is there sadness of heart? Is there discouragement? Whatever our lot, His consolations of love will see us through to the end. May we appropriate them today.

> *"Great legacy He left His own,*
> *'Twas left to them, to them alone;*
> *The peace which He Himself had known.*
>
> *This peace would keep us every day,*
> *'Midst all the world's distracted fray;*
> *We may possess it now—alway.*
>
> *No effort brings it out our door;*
> *Nor need we for its wealth implore;*
> *'Tis ours; exhaustless in its store.*
>
> *How comes it? Well, 'My peace I give.'*
> *'Tis ours as we His Word believe;*
> *It keeps—as we its wealth receive."*

When the consolations were finished, the Saviour said, *"Ye have heard how I said unto you, I go away, and come again unto you. If you loved Me, you would rejoice, because I said, I go unto the Father; for My Father is greater than I."* Let us love Him; let us rejoice that He is with the Father and enjoy His consolations until He returns. He is at home, with His Father; and we shall be there very soon!

—John W. Bramhall, July-August 1993, pp. 6-7

12. Shut Out

e were flying at about thirty thousand feet in a kind of "cloud sandwich." A high layer above blocked out the stars. Beneath there was only a sea of utter darkness, unrelieved by a single spot of light. The synchronized monotone of the four powerful engines was almost hypnotic. As I looked out into the night, I wondered what total absence of light would be. Reaching out, I turned down the rheostat switch that controlled the instrument panel lights. Utter, gross darkness enveloped us! A darkness that was almost tangible like a velvet shroud, a sable ink filling the eye sockets. Nothing could be seen.

Then came those words to mind, *"The blackness of darkness forever"* (Jude v. 13). Quickly I reached out and once again the flight deck was bathed in the gentle glow of the instruments. A few moments of that was enough for me! I glanced over at the co-pilot. Not a word had escaped his lips; he was staring silently ahead. We talked about that black moment and eternal realities, and he seemed to be moved, for a little, then reverted back to his usual chatter as though it was nothing.

Hell and outer darkness are not popular subjects. Indeed, for any who will preach it, it is profoundly distressing—and it ought to be. To think of a human soul shut out from God at last, from all light, and bound in the dark cell of a lost eternity is something we can hardly bear to think about.

Intellectual light is illumination of the mind. Spiritual light is revelation to the soul. Moral light is the reflection of holiness in the life. Visible light will be the manifestation of glory forever.

No light? In outer darkness, sight is an eternal futility with nothing to see. Thought is an eternal insanity without the light of the knowledge of God. The deathless worm of an unfading memory will recall, in useless remorse, the witness of a moral light that shone in holy lives which glorified the Father by good works and words. The darkness of eternal despair will settle upon the soul that has discovered too late it has missed the glory for which it was created.

Some mock hell and jokingly consign their friends to go there, thinking it is some kind of Las Vegas or Hollywood, the ultimate sin-pit with no restraints. But hell is a prison (2 Pet. 2:4). In hell there is no place to go, nothing to do but remember, and no one to sympathize or care.

Some would dismiss the teaching of hell as "barbaric" and claim that a "loving God would never send anyone to hell." First of all, let it be clearly understood that *"God is not willing that any should perish."* But *"All have sinned," "The wages of sin is death,"* and *"After death, the judgement"* are also facts of Scripture. People, because of their sins, are on the road to a lost eternity. It is God who has done everything to *keep them from perishing*, even to giving His beloved Son up to the cross to make a way of escape (Jn. 3:16).

Yet, like my old co-pilot, multitudes may have a serious moment or two, and then dismiss their thoughts of danger. "It'll never happen to me," they laugh. Well, sad to say, the Lord tells of some who will never make it into the light of heaven. Remember, these are the words of the compassionate Saviour, the Man of Sorrows, who died to save us. But if we will not have His mercy, there is no way to avoid the projection of our own choice. Live without Christ, die without Him, and spend that unthinkable conscious eternity without Him.

The Saviour tells of three kinds of people who will never make it to heaven. They are the *disbelieving* (Jn. 3:36), the *disobedient* (2 Thess. 1:7-8, Acts 17:30-31), and the *deceived* (Lk. 13:24-28).

Saddest of that pathetic army of the lost are those who expected to be in heaven, but are shut out. The Lord Jesus tells us in Luke 13 why they expected to enter in, but couldn't. First, they could use *religious language: "Lord, Lord"* (v. 25). Next, they had had a *religious experience:* they had taken the bread and wine of communion (v. 26). Lastly, they had the finest *religious instruction* (v. 26b). But they were shut out! The Lord tells why.

They were *unknown in heaven* (v. 27; see Rev. 20:15). They were *unchanged on earth* (v. 27b). They loved their sin. Saddest of all, they were *unacceptable to the Lord* at last (v. 27).

He, whose word on earth was 'Come'
Has said 'Depart'–Go, lost one, go,

Join yon lost angels in their woe,
Reap the sad harvest thou didst sow,
Their prison is thy home!

Dear soul, beloved and died for, flee to Christ now from all your sins, and toys of dust, and man's religion. *"Believe on the Lord Jesus Christ, and thou shalt be saved"* (Acts 16:31).

—*J. Boyd Nicholson, Editorial, July-August 1993, p. 3*

13. God's Man to the Rescue

n Genesis 14, Abram heard that his *"brother"* was taken captive. Lot was only his nephew, but Abram never lost his sense of kinship with his fallen relative. Abram knew all about the deliberate choice Lot had made. It would have been so easy for him to say, "He made his choice; let him live with the results." It is easy for the Christian today to have the same sense of disdain for his fallen brother. We need to be careful not to join those who have fallen into error, yet to have a concern and love for them that will seek their rescue, even as Abram had.

Abram was dwelling among the oaks of Mamre. As far as he was concerned, there were three notable things about Mamre. He had entertained angels there; it was there he was promised a son outside of all natural possibility; and there he found the cave called Machpelah. In Mamre, Abram had fellowship with God and knew God's blessing. Even when he had to lay away the remains of his beloved Sara, he was able to put her to rest in the arms of eternal confidence. He did not rejoice in his flocks and servants and far expanding fields. He had higher things in mind. Yet, he never lost his love and concern for poor, fallen Lot.

The message of Lot's captivity and distress galvanized Abram to action. Abram—a picture of the believer that walks with God—had both the means and the inclination to effect a rescue. This reminds us that the Church today should have the same qualities. She is to dwell on a higher level than the carnal Christian. At the same time, she is to have the means—because of continuing fellowship with the Lord—to reach out and rescue the fallen saint. She could never do so if she were to join that saint in his sinful captivity.

Abram's preparation to rescue Lot was not a matter of a few hours. Note that he had trained his servants born in his house. How significant. This reminds us that the Church is to be a place where souls are born again. Then, it is to be a place where those same souls are raised and trained to be effective servants for Christ. Brethren, let us not forget our twofold mission: both to reach the lost and then to raise the children to spiritual manhood. For it is the well-trained servant who will follow his Lord in times of need. It is the well-trained servant who will be the effective rescuer of the fallen saint. This training, and this work, is a life-long mission. Abram knew that, and he prepared accordingly. His servants were not hirelings. They were not temporary help. They were men of his house, of his training, of his heritage. The essence of a spiritual assembly is the same today. It sees birth; it sees growth; it sees maturity; it has life-long and effective servants. Are you part of such a gathering?

Abram went forth by night. The work of the Lord still goes on today in the same realm. Surrounded by darkness, yet endowed with a mission which cannot await the light of day, the Christian servant goes forth to do what no one else can accomplish. For Abram and his servants smote the enemy, rescued Lot and recovered all. Total victory! They pursued all the way to the neighborhood of Damascus to achieve this. This was a significant journey, especially at night. It meant crossing a valley, fording the Jordan, mounting the heights that we now know as the Golan, pursuit through wilderness, finally to victoriously engage in battle, and all in the darkness of night.

It is still the same for the Christian warrior. He crosses valleys, fords rivers, ascends heights. He pursues through the forbidding darkness of an enemy-infested night. But, if his weapons are not carnal, if prepared by the Spirit of God, he still wins victories. He yearns after his fallen brethren and they are blessed by his efforts.

Upon his return, Abram met the king of Sodom and the king of Salem. Yes, the enemy was still lurking. The king of Sodom wanted to take Lot back with him; and, alas, it seems that Lot was willing enough. The king of Sodom said, *"Give me the souls."* Abram could not restrain Lot. He had done what he could. He had achieved the rescue. And again, poor foolish Lot made his choice. But the king of Salem was also there. His proclamation was, *"Blessed be Abram of the most high God."* Abram's work and victory were noted at the highest levels. The commendation came from the king of peace himself. The rescue, despite Lot's choice, was not in vain.

God still needs men who ride through the night to the rescue. They are prepared servants. They are faithful. To them goes the victory! The results may seem at times to be tenuous; the thanks received from earth may be nil. It is not recorded that Lot ever said "Thank you" to Abram. But the efforts of such servants are noted on high by no less than the Prince of Glory Himself. The victories are never forgotten. The ultimate rewards are sure. Are you one of Abram's servants?

—Doug Kazen, July-August 1994, p. 8

14. They Shall Shine as the Stars

I f ever I saw a shining face I did that day! It was in central Africa at a conference meeting where many believers had come from villages far and near, some walking two days carrying bundles, babies and Bibles to hear the Word. The meetings were long. The insatiable appetite of the Christians for the Word was only exceeded by their joy that they could come together in this way. To find so many open ears and open hearts made it a delight to serve the Lord and His people by ministering the Word.

That face! "Shining" is the only word to describe him. He was sitting right in the center of the gathered company, beaming as the Word went forth.

At the close of the session, I asked one of the missionaries who that man was with the shining face. "Oh, that's Kambungu—I'll tell you his story later when we have a little time to talk."

His story went back many years. When he was a young man, one of the pioneer missionaries to those parts went through and spoke to the people from the book of Genesis. As he read the Scriptures aloud, the missionary came to the verse, *"Cursed is the ground for thy sake; in sorrow shalt thou eat of it all the days of thy life; thorns also and thistles shall it bring forth...in the sweat of thy face shalt thou eat bread"* (Gen. 3:17-19).

Those words, strangely enough, seemed to pierce Kambungu's heart. "That Book is right," he thought. "That is what I have to do, in the sweat of my face, every day in my field. I must find out what else that Book has to say." So, enquiring earnestly of the missionary, he learned God's way of salvation through faith in the Lord Jesus Christ and His redeeming work on the cross. His heart was open to the gospel and Kambungu was born again, a child of God.

He lived by the mighty Zambezi River where the lands of the Chokwe, the Lunda, and the Luvale peoples come together, speaking three different languages. It is a strategic spot for the spread of the gospel.

Kambungu wanted now to reach others with the gospel. So he decided he would work in his field in the morning. In the afternoons he would get into his dugout canoe and, with a bag of tracts, he would call on the villages along the river's edge.

However, Kambungu had a problem—he could not read. He did not want to be handing out tracts in the wrong language to the people. So he got hold of an old well-worn leather bag with three sections inside and had the missionary put the different language tracts each into a separate section so that he would know which was which.

Through the years, this beloved servant of the Lord faithfully labored by canoe up and down the great Zambezi River, and heaven alone will disclose the harvest of souls that will be his *"crown of rejoicing"* in *"that day."* Kambungu is now with the Lord, in the radiant glory he had seen only by faith and with the eyes of the heart.

In these western lands, the values of the world have a way of infiltrating the Church. The world says: "The man on the stage is the star!" Too often we can begin to think like the world: "The preacher on the platform is the star." Praise, plaudits, and position can be rendered to the public gifts. Therein lies a great danger, when men are given undue prominence and their words are given weight beyond the Scriptures themselves.

In 1 Corinthians 12, the gifts are likened to parts of the body, There are the visible gifts: ears, eyes, hands, feet. These are the *"comely"*—the elegant, well-formed—members, all contributing to the *harmonious function* of the whole. But, we are told, these have no need of *"more abundant honor"* (v. 24). Then there are the hidden gifts, likened to the internal organs of the body, having no particular elegance nor beauty to the eye. Yet these are vital to *the health* of the whole body.

While we would not wish it, we could do without a hand, an eye, an ear, a foot, and still have good bodily health. But the heart and the other life-sustaining organs, though not by any means "elegant" to the eye, functioning quietly, spontaneously, and out of sight, are *"necessary"* (v. 22).

It is wise and indeed incumbent on all those with public gift (whose gift, in any case is no praise to them, being sovereignly imparted by the Lord of the churches) when they rise to serve, to remember this: among those seated before them are silent sisters and quiet brethren whose function is out of the public eye, but who are familiar with the sanctuary. By their wise and quiet ministry, they are the real *"stars,"* turning many to righteousness (Dan. 12:3).

Actually their ministry is not so anonymous as they might think. Upon these, the well-known in the holy place who behold by faith the glory of the Lord, He invests the ministry of the shining face, *"from glory to glory."*

—*J. Boyd Nicholson, Editorial, July-August 1995, p. 3*

15. ALTOGETHER LOVELY

he word *"countenance"* in Song of Solomon 5 may be more accurately translated "bearing." *"His bearing is as Lebanon, excellent as the cedars."* Lebanon was high ground. The cedars of Lebanon were of great height, tall in a lofty excellence. The symbolism is very beautiful and of easy interpretation. This is Christ in the excelling dignity of His unique Manhood. Wherever we see Him, however we contemplate Him, His bearing is as Lebanon, excellent as those towering cedars.

The Gospels abound with portraits of Christ. We see Him as a Boy. We trace His pathway as a Man. We see Him with individuals and we see Him with the multitudes. We see Him with friends and with enemies. We see Him in the towns and in the villages, in the cities and in the wilderness, on the mountainside and by the lakeshore. We see Him with children and with the elders, with priests and with soldiers, before a Jewish king and before a Roman governor. But it matters not where we observe Him, it is always to admire One whose bearing is as Lebanon, excellent as the cedars. Perhaps this is why we so often read of Him as being *"in the midst."* He is predominant, preeminent, supreme and excelling, fairer than the children of men.

Have we sufficiently noticed His dignity as a Boy, when, having lost Him, His parents found Him in the temple in Jerusalem? Note that they found Him *"sitting...in the midst"* of the teachers of the law. A Boy of twelve years; a Galilean Boy from the despised Nazareth; sitting, at ease, in the midst of those learned doctors of Jewry, in earnest converse with them. Truly as we see Him there we may say, *"His bearing is ...excellent."*

And what of Him who, some eighteen years later, sat on the well at Shechem, the Man of Sychar. Alone He sat and talked with that woman of Samaria. Such a thing was not done in Judaism. Men did not converse in public with women. It was not permitted even for a man to talk with his wife in a public place. The disciples marvelled that He talked with a woman. (Not *"the"* woman, but *"a"* woman;

see JND). Yet, says John, no one questioned Him. There was a holy dignity with the Man of Sychar. The woman knew it too. *"Come,"* she exclaimed to the men of her city, *"Come, see a Man...!"* He was not as other men. He was excellent as the cedars.

Again and again throughout the course of His ministry, there are scenes of incomparable beauty where the excellency and dignity of Christ are evident. Sometimes He is teaching, sometimes healing, sometimes praying. At times He is in the synagogue, at times in some humble fisherman's cottage. It was a constantly gracious ministry which was always characterized by that holy bearing until at last they arrested Him in the garden.

They came with lanterns and torches and weapons. Lanterns and torches? On the night of a full Passover moon? Did they think that He would shrink from them, hiding amid the groves of Olivet? Weapons? Did they know Him so insufficiently as to imagine that the meek and lowly One would resist arrest and fight? O listen to His words and see His bearing in Gethsemane. *"Whom seek ye?...I am He...Let these go their way."* He stands in lofty excellence among them. They are confused; He is composed. His bearing is as Lebanon.

In the night that followed, He was arraigned before priests and elders, scribes and Sanhedrin. They bound Him, mocked Him, and falsely accused Him. They smote Him on the cheek and spat on His face. His disciples forsook Him. One of them denied Him. But He endured it all with incomparable dignity. That disciple who denied Him afterwards wrote, *"When He was reviled, He reviled not again."* In the house of Caiaphas, He stood excellent as the cedars in His calm and holy bearing.

The morning which followed that dark night brought increased suffering and sorrow. He was delivered to the Gentiles. Judaism clamored for His death by crucifixion, but they needed Roman approval. The Romans stripped Him, scourged Him, crowned Him with thorns and spat on Him as the Jews had done. They proclaimed His innocence, yet condemned Him to die. *"Behold the Man,"* cries the Governor. *"His bearing is as Lebanon,"* the saints reply, *"excellent as the cedars."* They crucified Him.

Three days later, He stands in another garden. His tomb is empty.

He leaves the grave clothes empty too, still in their folds as they had been wrapped around Him, but tenantless, no body now. He stands in the garden as the Jerusalem sun rises to a new and wondrous day. A weeping woman stands in the garden with Him, She turns as she hears His voice, *"Mary."*

—J. M. Flanigan, November-December 1993, p. 4

16. Tower of Tears

tanding starkly where the canal system of old Amsterdam exits near the Oosterdok is the Tower of Tears. It was the place where wives, mothers, and loved ones climbed to watch their sailor-men quietly slip away into the embrace of the dark ocean beyond. These were the weepers who caught their last glimpse of loved faces and waved farewell to those who were as dear as life itself. They watched as the ships of the famous "Flying Dutchmen" unfurled their sails to catch the winds that would take them around the Horn of Africa to the Indies and the faraway land which only by report was known.

These were the heroes of home who wiped their tears and returned to pick up the threads of life, to do their best till the time of separation would be over. Their anchors never dropped into blue lagoons in faraway tropic isles. Theirs was the stuff of life, the daily toil and the care of others. They did not set their course by the stars, but by the cobbled streets and well-worn paths of the crowded city. It was not theirs to climb the mast-head and shout "Land Ahoy!" It was theirs to wait…and wait…and wait, until the Great Return, the Grand Reunion, when even the tears of joy would be wiped away.

As we passed along the waterway and spied the old building that had heard the sob of separations, I look out my pen and jotted on the map edge, "Tower of Tears–Editorial. *'We sorrow not as others.'*"

At the end of the year, we say farewell to days we have lived and loved and left, days that will not return again. Must we climb the Tower of Tears and weep at their departure? Remorse is a pain no medicine can cure. Ours is but to cast ourselves again on the mercy of our God and seek for our foolish—but forgiven—past the grace to forget *"those things which are behind."*

There are hallowed memories that regale the mind and heart with joy and renew our strength again. David, disquieted and downcast, calls upon his soul to remember the God of "the Descender," Jordan, of the refreshing dews of Hermon, and of the delineations of *"the little hill"* (Ps. 42:6, margin).

58

Oh, what sacred memories there are for the child of God! Memories of the "Descender," the One who came down to the river of death. There to make it possible that brethren may dwell together in a unity as refreshing as the dew of Hermon. To remember week by week particularly that "little hill" where broke the storm of eternity upon the Lonely Sufferer (v. 7).

Then there are the memories that seem to rise up at this time of the year perhaps more than at other times, memories of our own Tower of Tears when we bade farewell to those who lived in our hearts. They set sail and went off without our permission to *the land of far distances.*" We took our last long, loving look into the faces we had grown accustomed to. But we too had to turn with breaking hearts back to the daily round and pick up the threads of life. We sorrowed, but *"not as others who have no hope."*

Oh, thank God for that! What a hope we have!

It is THE HOPE OF RESURRECTION AND RAPTURE. What a mystery! *"We shall not all sleep."* There are those of the saints who will never die, and we well may be that company who will never feel the killing sting nor surrender to the grave's victory.

It is the HOPE OF REVELATION AND REUNION. What a moment! More brief than the single throb of an insect's wing, more instant than a pulse of starlight or the thrum of a harper's string. We *"shall see His face!"* The artist's pigment will disintegrate before the blazing radiance and exquisite beauty of our glorious Lord. Reunion? Will we meet again those loved of long ago? David expected to see his child again. The sisters of Bethany were told *"Thy **brother** shall rise again."* Moses and Elijah were recognized on the mount. Relationships cannot be the same in heaven; they will be transformed, but not cancelled.

It is THE HOPE OF RE-FORMATION AND RESEMBLANCE. What a miracle! *"We shall be changed."* Changed as the corn of wheat is changed to the full head, in hundred-fold of what it was. *"We shall be like Him; for we shall see Him as He is."*

As we bid farewell to passing years, may we not be in "the Tower of Tears" but in the anticipation of triumph. As we remember loved ones who set sail for glory and are anchored safe in that haven of rest, may we thank God that they are *"far better,"* settled dwellers in the land that has no Tower of Tears in its harbor.

> *I know not what the future hath*
> *Of marvel or surprise,*
> *Assured alone that life and death*
> *His mercy underlies.*
> *And if my heart and flesh are weak,*
> *To bear the untried pain,*
> *The bruiséd reed He will not break,*
> *But strengthen and sustain.*
> *I know not where His islands lift,*
> *Their fronded palms in air,*
> *I only know I cannot drift*
> *Beyond His love and care.*

(John Greenleaf Whittier)

—J. Boyd Nicholson, Editorial, November-December 1993, p. 3

17. HOPE FOR THE SLANDERED

 lander. Diabolical in its origin. Determined in its intent. By evil design in its execution. Destructive in its effect. Mere gossip fades by comparison in its degree of evil. The Scriptures are unambiguous in their renunciation of slander. Its practice is clearly forbidden for the believer (Jas. 3). While it can be expected from the world (Jn. 15:20-21), it is alarming that it is practiced by believers. Slander burns a trail of sorrow, leaving behind saints and their service in apparent ruin.

But there is hope for the slandered. The person guilty of slander can make no such claim.

THE SLANDERED ARE IN NOBLE COMPANY

They say misery loves company, and the slandered find themselves among heaven's finest. Moses was a victim of slander. David, Paul, the Lord Jesus, and God Himself were slandered. It seems a strange pattern that the choicest of God's servants should be subject to such abuse. Yet this is the record. The slandered are tempted to feel their ministries are finished, but the sovereign God is not thrown off course by mere slander. He allows the finest to be slandered.

THE SLANDERED WILL BE VINDICATED EVENTUALLY

One of the great burdens of the slandered is the injustice of the whole thing. Unsubstantiated and false charges are free from scrutiny to prove their veracity. No evidence is ever demanded of the slanderer. They seem free to manufacture lies without restraint.

But there is vindication. Some will see vindication in their lifetime. Moses saw this as God moved quickly with Miriam and Aaron (Num. 12). David too saw his kingdom restored; he died renowned as the greatest king of Israel (1 Chron. 29:26-28).

Some see vindication in time, but not in their lifetime. The apostle Paul endured slander (2 Cor. 10:2, 10). At the end, he sadly records how all forsook him (2 Tim. 1:15; 4:10). Yet God would vindicate his life and ministry (1 Cor. 4). His unnamed accusers have faded, but we are indebted to the apostle for his authoritative epistles. There is no doubt he was God's man in the right place and at the right time.

Others will see vindication in eternity. This is the case with the Lord Jesus. While believers—in the minority—bow the knee now, ultimately in a future day, every knee will bow and every tongue confess that Jesus Christ is Lord to the glory of God the Father (Phil. 2:10-11).

So too with God: *"that God may be all in all,"* says the apostle (1 Cor. 15:28). God Himself will be vindicated in the consummation of the ages. The Christian echoes the closing words of Revelation: *"Even so, come, Lord Jesus."*

THEY WILL SEE VENGEANCE EXECUTED RIGHTEOUSLY

Vengeance is a powerful tool. It can only be trusted to the skilled expert. No novice should attempt vengeance. We cannot control what we start in seeking revenge. Happily for us, God has relieved us of that responsibility and assumes the responsibility for vengeance Himself (Rom. 12:17-21). No doubt Paul was thinking of this when he referred to Alexander the coppersmith (see 2 Tim. 4:14-15).

In fact, as if to add insult to injury, the slandered are invited to pray for their enemies. This is high level Christianity, but it has proven results. This kind of praying has as much an effect and blessing on us as it does for those who oppose us. It is said of Job, *"The Lord turned the captivity of Job, when he prayed for his friends"* (Job 42:10). Some friends. Some prayer.

THEY ARE ENCOURAGED TO GO ON FAITHFULLY

The worldly slogan, peppered with truth, says, "When the going gets tough, the tough get going." Although the slandered feel devastated and are tempted to give up or give in, they must not do so. God has special provision for them. David's reflections in Psalm 31 speak to the slandered. His experience with slander and the Holy Spirit's movement on David to write, gives the slandered wise, authoritative, and comforting counsel.

David says, *"For I have heard the slander of many: fear was on every side: while they took counsel together against me, they devised to take away my life"* (v. 13). Again, *"Thou shalt hide them in the secret of Thy presence from the pride of man: Thou shalt keep them secretly in a pavilion from the strife of tongues"* (v. 20). Read the entire psalm and notice David's trust and God's promise.

The slandered. Sadly, they are a growing number among us. But God does not abandon the slandered. He will take the evil of slander and make it praise Him. There is such a hope for the slandered.

—Brian Gunning, July-August 1995, p. 4

18. GOD BLESS THE GIBLITES!

Listed by Asaph in Psalm 83 among the fiercest enemies of Israel, the Ammonites, the Amalekites, and the Philistines, this little known people came from the town of Gebal (later Byblos) a Phoenician seaport between Sidon and Tripolis. They with the others were to be driven out and their land divided, but somehow it seems they never were (Josh. 13:5-6).

They were skilled craftsmen, but of rather an inglorious trade, working mostly out of sight, yet their labors were essential to the finished project. King Hiram discovered them and engaged their services and then, in spite of their past association with the enemies of Israel, commissioned them to Solomon, who received them to help in building the temple.

There are four things we can discover about them. They were *"stoppers of chinks"* (Ezek. 27:9, marg.). Being men of the seaport, where shipbuilding was a thriving industry, they had the rather menial task of working underneath the boats, caulking the joints between the planks. But how vital this was to the seaworthiness of the vessel. They made sure their ships would not spring a leak. Seaworthy vessels they would be, and their crews likely had no idea who the Giblites were.

They were also *"squarers of stones"* (1 Ki. 5:18) when Solomon's temple was being built. Remembering that the cutting, shaping, and finishing of the stones was all done out of sight and out of hearing for *"there was neither hammer nor axe nor any tool of iron heard in the house"* (1 Ki. 6:7).

Another thing we learn about the Giblites is that they *"strengthened the structure"* (Ezek. 27:9, marg.). Whether stone or timber, on land or on sea, their work was a work of strengthening.

We can discover something further about them, from the meaning of their name. It is derived from *gabal,* meaning to set bounds. These Giblites were also "setters of boundaries."

How interesting to find this people, once enemies of God's people and under God's judgment, now serving Him and His people, commissioned to work on the building of the house of the Lord. Had they known the words, their favorite hymn as they cut, sawed, shaped, and fitly framed the costly stones together could well have been "Amazing Grace!"

God bless the Giblites; how we thank God for those laborers today, the *"helps"* (1 Cor. 12:28), who can work out of sight and seek no glory for themselves, if only they can be "stoppers of chinks." They can discern those danger spots in our lives where the world can seep in, ever enlarging the chink, ever rotting the plank. By their skilled and timely intervention, a word of warning, a word of instruction or loving exhortation, they plug the danger spots and we are preserved from shipwreck. It may be a word of godly rebuke as these "stoppers of chinks" pack the caulking of God's Word into our conscience. Not comfortable perhaps, but *"faithful are the wounds of a friend"* and God in His grace uses those humble servants—a brother here, a sister there—to preserve us from disaster.

God bless the Giblites who without fanfare, work away at shaping and fitting the living stones in the building of God. They can smooth the rough edges—if we have grace and sense to let them. They well know these stones are, as in Solomon's temple, *"costly"* and *"precious"* and they use their gifts to beautify the saints. They labor that we may *"dwell together in unity"* for we are *"living stones."*

God bless the Giblites who know how to *"strengthen the things that remain"* and how to *"strengthen thy brethren."* They are strong in the Lord for they have discovered that His work is done, not by might or power, but by His Spirit.

God bless the Giblites; who know where "the boundaries" are. Familiar with the Sacred Documents that set out those boundaries, they warn us if they see us wandering away. They raise the warning signs at the door to the downward path, *"Love not the world neither the things that are in the world"—"Come out from among them and be ye separate and touch not the unclean thing."*

God bless the Giblites; what a debt we owe them. Where would some of us have been today but for those stoppers of chinks, squarers of stones, strengtheners of the structure and setters of boundaries? Yet behind their unheralded labor is the eternal purpose of the One whose temple we are.

Little did those ancient Giblites realize their name would be written in the Word of God and their work recorded. Though unnoticed and often unappreciated down here, the books will be opened and due reward appointed to them. God *will* bless "the Giblites" for their unique service, their labor of love, and their care for the people of God.

We who have been blessed by their counterparts in the Church will thankfully rejoice at their reward and say, "God bless the Giblites!"

—J. Boyd Nicholson, Editorial, January-February 1996, p. 3

19. Behold What Love! (Jn. 7:31)

o God only wise, it is entirely fitting that a subject near to every believer's heart is also furthest from his or her comprehension. God is love, and that love is therefore as unfathomable as God Himself. Yet we delight to plumb the depths of that love over and over to see if we can gain even a little better sounding of it.

Such an attribute of our great God and Saviour continues to draw us to Him like bees to the sweetest clover. Letting down the plumb line in a few places gives us five views of His love to rejoice over.

The Manner of It

John invites us to behold the manner of love that the Father has bestowed upon us (1 Jn. 3:1). His emphasis in this expression is that this love is from another country, a foreign land. That country is heaven, and its love is as foreign to what we call love as a jewel of gold is to the snout of a pig. That is the picture that Proverbs uses when it suggests how out of place it is to see a fair woman with an ugly disposition. They are two things that just don't belong together. This love that God sent to us in His Son is a love we can never deserve. It seems misplaced. It is a love that is alien to every experience of this world.

The heart of this love is developed in this way: First, there is the calling or naming of the beloved as the children of God. Missing from the KJV are the added words in verse 1, after this calling, "and so we are" to emphasize that we were named children of God from heaven when we received the eternal life that was with the Father but brought to us through Christ. Second, there is an immediate separation from the world, for the world knows not God. Third, to contrast the first two, there is the wonder of our ultimate manifestation as children of God, when we meet the Lord who loved us.

Finally, there is the purifying power of a hope grounded in such a love. It is miraculous that God could ever love us so. Yet this love did come, and it came to us in *"the fulness of the time"* (Gal. 4:4).

THE MOMENT OF IT

It would surely be manifest at that moment when God's giving reached its pinnacle. God commended His love toward us *"in that while we were yet sinners, Christ died for us"* (Rom. 5:8). Paul says that after such a giving as this, believers may be sure that God will freely give us all things. In giving His Son for us, He has already given the greatest, so all other gifts are small by comparison.

As with its manner, there is a sharp contrast here. God commends His love even while we are sinners. There is nothing in sin or sinners to draw God's love out. The way we practice love is different. A boy meets a girl and some attraction draws out their love. But sin and sinners are repulsive to God on the basis of their character. So they cannot commend themselves to God. Yet His love came freely out from His loving heart, and without any cause in us. The culmination of it was the death of Christ for us.

Of course God's love is not bound by a moment, though it was focused on the work of the cross. But Christ loved the Church first, and then He gave Himself for it. I cannot imagine there was a time when the eternal Son did not love the Church.

This contrast was there at the cross while God was commending that love in full. There was the awful hatred of the scribes and Pharisees. There was the callous indifference of the mob gathered for the spectacle. There was the intense despising of imperial Rome who ratified the order for the Saviour's crucifixion. What a contrast! Hateful hearts over against the Saviour's display of God's great heart of love, unconditionally commending that love to us. *"Father, forgive them, for they know not what they do."*

THE MEASURE OF IT

Can we measure the *"so"* of *"God so loved the world"*? Paul prayed that the Ephesians might know Christ "at home" in their hearts by faith, being rooted and grounded in love. He prayed that they might know its measure in all its breadth and length and depth and height. It is a love which passes knowledge and is intended to fill believers with the fullness of God (Eph. 3:17-19).

A poor man in Israel might sell himself to be a servant to pay his debt. But when the year of Jubilee came, he would go out free with a cancelled debt. He could be redeemed sooner if someone purchased him. The price would depend on the years remaining until the year of Jubilee.

Think of a servant who has reached the day before the year of Jubilee. What price to free him one day early? He says, "Forget it; I'll wait until tomorrow." But for a man who had five years to go, the price would of course be greater, but still less than the man who had 49 years to go.

Our case was different than these. If no Redeemer ever came, we were enslaved to sin's bondage forever. How perilous it would have been to wait until tomorrow! So if our servitude to sin was eternal without a redeemer, what price to redeem? The price was measured by His great love expressed, *"the precious blood of Christ."* The life behind that sacrifice, and nothing less will give the measure.

THE MYSTERY OF IT

The Lord Jesus has given each of His own the glory that the Father gave Him. That would be akin to His glory and not the unique glory of the Son, but it is still the glory the Father gave Him for us. It was given that we might know a unity such as the Father and the Son alone have always known. The key to such perfect oneness is Christ in us, and the Lord Jesus in the Father.

This gift demonstrates that the Father sent the Son to love us with the same love with which the Father loved Him (Jn. 17:23-24).

Many secret things of God have been revealed in the New Testament because the Son has come. They are called mysteries in Scripture. The character of this love is surely among them, even though God's love shown in the Old Testament was a towering love. In many ways it encompasses the mystery of godliness, the mystery of the Church, the mysteries of the kingdom, and the mystery of the rapture of the saints. They are all dependent on His love. In praise of such amazing love, Charles Wesley wrote:

'Tis mystery all! The immortal dies!
Who can explore His strange design?
In vain the first-born seraph tries
To sound the depths of love divine!

"Amazing love," indeed. While it is a mystery, within that mystery it is a marvelous love, too. Consider Gomer, the unfaithful wife of the prophet Hosea. He sustained and supported her even while she was committing adultery against him. Would it not enrage a man's heart to realize he gave his hard-earned money to a wife he loved so she could go away for the weekend with another man?

Eventually she was sold by her patrons as a slave. Standing in the slave market, perhaps finally sorrowing for her folly, there comes a marvel to this reprobate wife. In the hot noonday market, heavy with the odor of flesh for sale, she looks up to see her wronged husband, Hosea. He has been sent by the Lord with the simple charge, *"Go yet, love a woman beloved of her friend, yet an adulteress, according to the love of the Lord toward the children of Israel, who look to other gods, and love flagons of wine"* (Hos. 3:1).

He buys her and loves her, even in such a vile condition, and takes her again to himself. This marvel is a faint glimmer of the Lord Jesus coming to redeem us through the love of our God. It begins to tell the *"so"* of John 3:16. It is a mystery revealed under the darkness of Golgotha's brow where Jesus bowed His sacred head for all the Gomers of this world, and worse too!

THE MESSAGE OF IT

God's clarion call to this world has come through love. To every sinner it is to believe on the love shown through the giving and the sending of His Son for sin and sins. When the people asked the Lord Jesus how they could do the works of God, His answer was, *"This is the work of God, that ye believe on Him whom He hath sent"* (Jn. 6:29).

Every believer is to further that great work of God by continuing to believe and do good works for His glory, for faith without works is dead.

Believers are only made capable of love because the Lord Jesus first loved us (1 Jn. 4:19). The expression and reality of that love wherewith we have been loved, is the mark of His own people today. It marked out those who followed Him in His life as disciples. It marks out those who are now participating in His glorious life today. *"Beloved, if God so loved us, we ought also to love one another"* (1 Jn. 4:11).

—David B. Robins, July-August 2000, pp. 8–9

20. WHAT ARE WE DOING HERE ANYWAY?

f the Lord Jesus had wanted us only to be holy and happy forever, why did He not take us right into heaven the moment we were saved? Think of the tears, the trials, and the temptations we would never have known. What displeasing of the Father, what offending of the Saviour, what grieving of the loving, patient, longsuffering Holy Spirit we would never have caused! Why did He leave us here in this world? Just what is the point? The world! That's the point! But what do we, the people of God, have to do with *the world*?

In that Mount Everest chapter of the Bible, John 17, where the air is pure, the clatter of the world and the smoke of battle are never known. It is the silence of the sanctuary. There, *"Jesus lifted up His eyes to heaven."* We tremble even to listen to the voice of the Master in intimate communion with His Father and can almost hear, out of the realms of holy fire, the words, *"...put off thy shoes from off thy feet, for the place whereon thou standest is holy ground."* Yet hear we must, for it is recorded that we might listen to the mighty intercessions of the Son of God for His own beloved who are *"in the world."*

Seven times the Saviour speaks to the Father about His own and their relationship to *"the world."* First they are seen as *a gift out of the world*. To think of the Father giving His beloved Son to us is beyond us. But that the Father would present us to His Son as a gift leaves us utterly baffled.

The Saviour was soon to finish His mighty work and leave the world, but His own would be *left in the world*. Left in this evil realm—but, He has told them, not alone. He will not leave them *"orphans."*

He prays to the Father for their preservation because they will soon be identified as aliens by their lifestyle and likeness to Himself. It will be evident that *they are not of the world*.

The light of their lives will rebuke and convict the world and its dark and devious ways, so they should not be surprised that they will be *hated by the world*.

In the light of all this, the Lord Jesus prays not for their isolation but their insulation, that they might be *kept from the world*.

Now as we hear the Saviour's mighty intercession we are full of wonder. In the great and eternal purpose *He sends them into the world!* Why? His lambs among the wolves? The children among the lions? His beloved sent into the battlefield against the forces of hell? Almost in pain, we ask again, Why?

He leaves us wondering no longer why He left us here and why He sends us into the world that crucified Him and hates Him still. It is so that others *"shall believe on Me through their word"* and that by their oneness with Him *"the world may believe."*

So that is why He left us here! He still loves the world of sinners. So, He will tell His own again, as His last command before leaving and being *"received up into heaven," "Go ye into all the world and preach the gospel to every creature."*

It is a master stroke of the enemy that he has diverted many of the Lord's people from this clear command. He has subtly changed the frequency of their hearing, so they no longer receive God's emergency calls. The enemy doesn't look so terrible; so why fight him? Our swords are nicely polished and handsomely displayed. Our trumpets have been laid down. They were so crude, and anyway they gave such an uncertain sound the people didn't bother.

The cross? The blood? Judgment? Hell, where the fire is never quenched? Parching thirst that is never relieved? The undying worm of a flawless memory? Isolation in the blackness of a darkness—forever, and forever, and forever? Surely we can't disturb and distress people with such barbaric notions, can we? Let's just all talk about love!

No one loved humankind like the Man of Sorrows. Yet He is the very One who raises the warning cry. He it was who went into the abyss alone to save us from that lost eternity. It is that love that warns!

There is no message like it. It comes out of the heart of God. It is the *only* message on the face of the earth with concrete promises and absolute assurances. It sweeps across every barrier man has raised of color, language, education, and privilege. It offers pardon from sin and the gift of eternal life that brings us into the knowledge of God, so that we might fulfill the reason for our existence: His glory! It is the gospel of the glory of the blessed God.

Why is it, then, that in some assemblies this glorious gospel is hardly ever clearly preached? Why are we not shouting it from the housetops? Why are we not gossiping it among our neighbors? Why are we not nurturing our children in it and blessing the aged with its hope and glory? Why are we not fulfilling the reason we have been left in the world?

Maybe we just don't believe it!

—*J. Boyd Nicholson, Editorial, November-December 1999, p. 3*

21. HIS PEACE (JN. 16:33)

ohn 16 provides our Lord's last recorded words to His disciples before His trial and crucifixion. There is nothing men desire more than peace, and nothing so elusive. So many things disrupt our peace, both at home and in the world. One soldier was so hounded by his wife that he wrote her, "Why won't you let me fight this war in peace?"

Peace cannot be found in circumstances, because our circumstances are as changeable as the weather. Peace can only be found in the Lord of our circumstances, for our times are in His hands—both good and bad times, for He has set prosperity and adversity over against one another. In both, there are profitable lessons to be learned.

The Psalmist declared: *"It was good for me that I was afflicted. Before I was afflicted I went astray."* Job exclaimed: *"When I am tried, I shall come forth as gold."* We read in Proverbs: *"The fining pot is for silver, and the furnace for gold."* God is glorified in the trials through which He brings us. Daniel's three friends were different men as the result of their fiery experience.

> *When through fiery trials thy pathway shall lie,*
> *My grace, all-sufficient, shall be thy supply.*
> *The flames shall not hurt thee; I only design,*
> *Thy dross to consume, and thy gold to refine.*

We read in Hebrews 12,

Whom the Lord loveth He chasteneth, and scourgeth every son whom He receiveth...Now no chastening for the present seemeth to be joyous, but grievous: nevertheless afterward it yieldeth the peaceable fruit of righteousness unto them which are exercised thereby.

The Word of God affirms: *"Thou wilt keep him in perfect peace, whose mind is stayed on Thee...Trust ye in the Lord forever: for in the Lord Jehovah is everlasting strength."* "When all around my soul gives way, He then is all my hope and stay."

Did He not leave His own a legacy of peace? *"Peace I leave with you, My peace I give unto you: not as the world giveth, give I unto you. Let not your heart be troubled, neither let it be afraid."*

As they were assembled for fear of the Jews hind shut doors, Jesus came and stood in the midst, saying, *"Peace be unto you;"* and when He had said this, He showed them His hands and side, "blest emblems of the Crucified."

What a paradox it is that the mightiest work ever accomplished was done when the Saviour was nailed to the tree! Peter writes that *"Who His own self bare our sins in His own body on the tree."* Paul writes that He took that which was against us out of the way, nailing it to His Cross.

It was while He hung on the Cross that He cried, *"It is finished!"* not *"I am finished!"*

He first showed them His hands, for He had the power to do the work; and then He showed them where the spear had pierced His side, to tell us that, without the shedding of blood, there is no forgiveness of sin, and that He loved us and gave Himself for us. Yes, blessed be His Name, He made peace for us *"by the blood of His cross."*

Then He said to them again, *"Peace be unto you; as My Father hath sent Me, even so send I you."* He has called believers out of this world to be His own, and He has sent us back into the world to declare the gospel to all people. He then breathed on them to let them know that, through His Spirit, He would provide the power needed for Christian life and witness. He told them later to wait in Jerusalem until they were endued with the power of the Spirit of God. *"Ye shall receive power after that the Holy Ghost shall come upon you, and ye shall be witnesses unto Me in Jerusalem, Judea, Samaria, and the uttermost parts of the earth."*

He put them in trust with the gospel and empowered them by His Spirit to carry the message of the glory of Christ everywhere. They had divine authority to proclaim to all men life and blessing through His Name; and to warn all Christ-rejecters and neglecters of their awful fate.

But Thomas, one of the twelve, was absent when Jesus came. He missed seeing the Saviour; he rejected the testimony of apostles. The

Lord said to him later, *"Because ye have seen, ye have believed. Blessed are they that have not seen, and yet have believed."* Peter writes, *"Though now we see Him not, yet believing, we rejoice with joy unspeakable and full of glory."*

—*Elliot Van Ryn, November-December 1997, p. 6*

22. HE MADE IT AGAIN

 poiled vessels! What a tragedy! Not just dropped on the floor, but *"marred in the hand of the potter."* The potter was at work on the clay. It wasn't just a "pot" he was making, it was a *"work on the wheels."* There was a design, a purpose, a place for the vessel. Then it happened, *"marred"*—the word means, spoiled, ruined, injured. That's it! Finished! Just garbage now, only good for "the potter's field" with all the rest of the broken vessels. Well, no, not exactly.

In the record of Jeremiah, where we read of this potter and the vessel (18:1-6), a shaft of light shines in the potter's house. There is the potter's heart. He will not leave that clay marred and wasted. So *"he returned,"* for by the desire of his heart and the ability of his hands there was hope of recovery and further usefulness. *"He made it again another vessel"* as seemed good to the potter.

What a message of hope and encouragement! Do you not wonder what our Heavenly Potter's original design was for us? Then when the work was marred, He did not throw us out to the potter's field, but took us up again into those wise and capable hands to make us again another vessel.

What about that vessel, Jacob? What design and purpose there was in that life. Then the marring! The stealing of the birthright, deceiving his old, blind father, fleeing from his rightful place. Finished? Well, no, the Lord's eye was upon him and He showered him with His goodness, for *"the goodness of God leadeth thee to repentance."*

At last, repentant, Jacob returned to put things right and the Divine Potter gets His hands on him again—all night, until he was back to the place where he was marred, *"I am Jacob."* Now hear the Divine Potter, *"...no more Jacob, but Israel: for as a prince hast thou power with God and with men..."* *"He made it again"* and *"the sun rose upon"* him. Jacob came out of that night (yes, limping—he will never walk the same again) another vessel, made again.

There is that lovely vessel, David, described in the catalog of the

Divine Potter as skillful in music, brave, prudent in speech, beautiful in his person. Then that sad day of the marring of the vessel. Finished now? No, not quite, The Divine Potter picks up the clay again and works on him in the joyless days of his remorse. What pressure of those hands, what work *"on the wheels"* till at last out of his anguish David cried to God alone, *"my transgressions...mine iniquity...my sin...this evil."* Then again he found the joy of his salvation, his silence turned to singing, the long drought turned into summer. Where sin abounded grace did much more abound. David becomes a picture of the Shepherd King in His beauty, and from Bathsheba, God gave him Solomon, a picture of the King in His glory. Made again, another vessel. What a wonderful Potter!

Peter was chosen by the Potter Himself to be a special vessel of mercy, of love, and grace. Then the marring. He warmed himself at the world's fire, *"for it was cold."* Never colder of body, never colder of heart, for *"Then began he to curse and to swear, saying, I know not the man."* Marred! Oh, that look of love from the Master, and he went out and wept bitterly. No doubt he remembered the words of the Lord Jesus, *"But whosoever shall deny Me before men, him will I also deny before My Father which is in heaven."* Finished now! No hope! Spoiled! Ruined?

Then came the morning. The sun rose, the earth warmed, the birds sang, for the grave could not hold the King! The heavenly messenger tells the women at the tomb, *"But go your way, tell His disciples and Peter..."* Oh! what a message for that broken vessel! He never forgot it. By this mighty resurrection his hope was revived, his fellowship was restored and his work was renewed. Chosen to preach at Pentecost! Another vessel, made again!

When we have sinned, how the enemy, as with Peter, desires to have us to sift us as wheat. He would make us feel we are finished for God—no more use, *"marred in the hand of the Potter."* But we are still in His hands, we are still on His heart, we are still in His house, and we are still in His hopes. The Divine Potter is not finished with us yet. He is able to make us again even at this late day. But the clay must be pliable. *"But now, O Lord, Thou art our Father; we are the clay, and Thou our potter; and we all are the work of Thy hand"* (Isa. 64:8).

As the Lord dealt with Peter privately, so it is between our souls and Him alone. Let us put that marred life into those loving, capable hands, and He will make us again another vessel as it pleases Him.

> *Come! Not to find, but make this heart*
> *A dwelling, worthy of Thee as Thou art,*
> *To chase the gloom, the terror, and the sin,*
> *Come! All Thyself, yea come, Lord Jesus,*
> *Do now come in.*

(Handley G. C. Moule)

—*J. Boyd Nicholson, Editorial, September-October 2000, p. 3*

23. High Sounding Nonsense

his article is especially for Christian young people who are at school or college. Every day you may sit under the instruction of unregenerate men and women who have no love for your Saviour or your Bible. At first, you are sure that you will not be affected by their anti-Christian teachings, but then you become caught by what I call "the illusion of the classroom." You begin to think: "This man must know what he is talking about. After all, he is a scholar." From this, it is an easy step to the conclusion that the Christians are a fairly ignorant lot, the elders do not know what is going on, and your parents are definitely back numbers. And how can we know that the Bible is the Word of God anyway? Listen! The Apostle Paul has a message for you: *"Be careful that nobody spoils your faith through intellectualism or high-sounding nonsense. Such stuff is at best founded on man's ideas of the nature of the world and disregards Christ"* (Col. 2:8, Phillip's translation).

The wise Christian is not taken in by the high-sounding nonsense of modem intellectualism. He is not terrified when he is called an "obscurantist." He refuses to bow at the shrine of man's wisdom. Instead, he realizes that in Christ are hidden all the treasures of wisdom and knowledge, and that since he has Christ he never needs to be ashamed of his faith. Because these teachers do not have Christ, he does not expect them to have the divine insight possessed by the humblest believers. He can listen to their teachings and calmly appraise them in the light of God's Word. If he finds any instruction which is opposed to the Scriptures, he rejects it. He casts down human reasonings and every high thing that exalts itself against the knowledge of God and brings every thought into captivity to the obedience of Christ (2 Cor. 10:5).

He does not expect his Bible to agree with the changing findings of science. Indeed, he is glad that the Bible does not agree with the many unproved theories he studies. Otherwise the Bible would have to change as frequently as the textbooks.

Unfortunately, not all Christian young people have this maturity of judgment. They have an excessive reverence for human wisdom and knowledge, and they come by it honestly because they have been fed it by their parents since they could first use big words.

Off they go to college and who is waiting for them but the devil himself? He uses the same tactic that he employed with Eve; he appeals to the mind. "You have such a brilliant intellect. You can go places in the world, but not so long as you are narrow enough to take the Bible literally. Now," he says, "what you want to do is to put the Bible to the test of human reason. If it is not reasonable, it cannot be true. Just examine it objectively and tell me how you can know that the Bible is God's Word."

History repeats itself. Eve fell for this line, and many of her sons and daughters are falling for it, too: *"But I fear, lest by any means, as the serpent beguiled Eve through his subtility, so your minds should be corrupted from the simplicity that is in Christ"* (2 Cor. 11:3).

Few things are more pathetic than a young believer who "goes intellectual." He loses the simplicity that is in Christ. The freshness of his early faith disappears. The Bible he once enjoyed no longer attracts him; he cannot read it without thinking of doubts and denials. He no longer has a song in his heart. As for witnessing for Christ, he has been stricken dumb like Zacharias, because he doubted the Word of the Lord. Too often he drifts away from Christian fellowship and wanders out into the darkness of a wasted life.

Is there anything a young Christian can do to guard against the peril of a spoiled faith?

First of all, he can obtain the Lord's guidance concerning the college he attends. In some he will find those who will help, in others he will find much opposition. Not all Christian young people can survive in an anti-Christian atmosphere, although a few succeed in emerging with a triumphant testimony.

Secondly, he should exercise prayerful discretion with regard to the courses he takes. If he thinks he can play with fire and not be burned, he knows more than the Bible. The Bible asks: *"Can a man take fire in his bosom, and his clothes not be burned?"* (Prov. 6:27). And the answer is clearly "No!"

Thirdly, he should spend time each day in the Word of God. Most cases of college cancer occur when critical theories of the Bible occupy the time that the Bible should have.

Fourthly, he should keep himself pure. I am convinced that most cases of apostasy result from moral failure rather than from honest intellectual difficulties.

Fifthly, he should seek Christian companionship at college and help other believers in making Christ known.

Finally, he should pray constantly that God will keep him from the defilement and pollution of godless philosophies, and preserve him for a life of usefulness and fruitfulness for Himself.

—William MacDonald, September-October 2000, pp. 10–11

24. THE SOUND OF A GENTLE STILLNESS

ell, yesterday we laid away the earthly remains of another of God's choice servants. I was saying to his beloved partner, this going home one at a time is a painful business. How we look forward to all going together, *"in a moment."*

Brother Tom Agnew had been an auto mechanic for many years. Not just a "fixer," but a man who put his Christian testimony into his workmanship, and nothing was too much trouble to make things right. His brother-in-law told us that one day he was having engine trouble and was apprehensive about even driving the old car to the repair shop. So he called Tom on the phone for help. "Start the engine," said Tom. "Now, put the phone in beside the engine for a minute." The problem was diagnosed "long distance" and the driver was assured it was quite safe to make the journey.

Later, Tom moved into sales and was renowned for many years as one of that unusual breed, a thoroughly trustworthy car salesman!

Every few years, when we were looking for a dependable machine, I would call Tom on the phone and ask him if he saw something we could use, to let us know. He understood just what we needed, and more than once I have bought a car from Tom over the phone, just on his word, sight unseen. Dealing with Tom, you didn't even need to kick the tires.

But I never heard him preach a sermon. He was a quiet brother, gentle and kind and full of the servant spirit, though unmoveable in his convictions and his commitment to the Lord and His Word.

As we stood by his grave yesterday, I was impressed again with the great value to the Church—and in testimony to the world—of the quiet gifts. I fear that far too much publicity and praise and prominence have been given to the public gifts.

It may come as a shock to some that when we read about the gifts in Scripture, the public gifts are not necessarily the most vital. In 1 Corinthians 12, we are told that gifts are given to people by God the Holy Spirit. These gifted persons have been set in the church, *"first apostles...,"* that is "first of all," in order. The gifts are likened to members of the body: the foot, the hand, the ear, and the eye. Now these are outward, each having their own place and function for all to see. They have their own singular position, particular beauty, and evident use, contributing to the whole body. But, valued as they are, they are not absolutely essential to the health of the body. A person can lose a hand, a foot, or an eye and otherwise still be in good health, though incomplete.

However, there are other gifts, likened to the hidden members of the body, not particularly *"comely"* nor in the public eye, but *"necessary"* for life and health and cannot be done without. So, such hidden organs as the heart and lungs are not considered particularly beautiful, but we deem them of *"more abundant"* value. We cannot do without them.

So the day to day health, strength, and welfare of the assembly is not dependent on the preachments of the gifted, wonderful though they may be, but rather on the continuing, quiet ministry of the silent gifts among us, ongoing through the years.

How can we evaluate the private prayers of godly sisters who through our life have breathed our names and needs into the ear of the Father? Or who can assess the worth of faithful men who bind the saints together with their private intercession and show by their demeanor the silent evidence of the fruit of the Spirit, though their voices are seldom if ever heard in public? How many of us still, after many years, draw upon resources poured into our lives by godly men and women who, like Priscilla and Aquila with Apollos, took us aside and *"expounded unto [us] the way of God more perfectly"*?

What wonderful surprises we will have at the Bema! Praying mothers who mingled their tears with their intercessions and faithfully raised their children for God will then receive their crown. Christ-like brethren who carried with them the fragrance of the sanctuary, and bore *"the infirmities of the weak,"* will hear the Lord's *"Well done."*

So, quiet brother, silent sister, who perhaps feel at times you have little to contribute to the ministry of the assembly, faint not! It is the daily breathing of the Spirit through you, the beating of the heart of the Master in you, that the Lord uses to maintain the ongoing health and vitality of the assembly, so that when the public gifts are exercised, the anointing of God will be upon the preaching, and open ears and hearts will be ready to receive the Word.

Well, Tom went home suddenly, and as we might have expected, quietly. But the large numbers from many parts that attended his funeral and stood silently by his grave attested to the truth that he, a quiet brother, *"being dead, yet speaketh."*

—J. Boyd Nicholson, Editorial, July-August 1997, p. 3

25. They Broke Through

hat heroic stories are outlined in David's roll of honor! It is like an advance edition of The Lamb's Book of Life. What deep organ music throbs in the sonorous Hebrew names of the mighty men: Eleazar, Abishai, Benaiah, Abiezer, Eliam, Hezrai, Hurai of the brooks of Gaash, Naharai, and then like the sound of a solemn discord, Uriah the Hittite. We miss valiant Ittai the Gittite and conclude that he must have fallen with his face to David's foes.

Among the noble deeds recorded there is one that stands out from the rest as an example of uttermost devotion, for three reasons: it is told in the greatest detail, it links together three brave men, and it withholds their names. They were merely three of the thirty chief, yet the lessons they teach us are of higher value than those of their comrades. They joined David's band, turning traitor to Saul or another master, to throw in their lot with the exile when his fortunes were at a very low ebb.

It was the hot month of harvest before the summer ends, when prudent men must prepare for the winter; but forsaking the inviting fields, they sought out David in his comfortless cave amid the fastnesses of the Judean hills. His ancient enemies, the Philistines, had invaded Judah and occupied Bethlehem. Saul, mad with rage and jealousy, was powerless to expel them. David, homesick, allowed a longing to escape from his lips for a drink from his village well, water cool and sweet and satisfying. How often in his boyhood days had he quenched his thirst and watered his flocks at that unfailing spring!

Not waiting for a word of command, as one man, the three slipped out of the hold to make their way through that rugged hill country to Bethlehem, intent on their forlorn hope. Not darkly at dead of night did they steal through the Philistine lines, passing like shadows by the sleepy sentinels; but *"they break through"* the astonished host with cyclonic fury, irresistible in their onslaught, their goal the well by the guarded gate. They reached it; one plunged a water skin into the depths, brought it up dripping, and then—cutting and thrusting, giving and taking wounds—they were gone.

So they returned to David, silently presenting their hard-won trophy. He saw that the simple gift represented three lives laid at his feet in love for him. The water was the symbol of their blood; he could not drink such a sacrificial thing. Suddenly, that rude hiding place became a sanctuary, as David lifted the water skin and slowly its precious contents trickled down to the thirsty ground. No voice said, *"To what purpose is this waste?"* for he said with awe: *"Be it far from me, O Lord, that I should drink this; is not this the blood of the men that went in jeopardy of their lives!"*

Only God was worthy of such a gift, so it must be presented to Him. What was intended to slake a passing thirst, made glad the heart of God, for with such sacrifices He is well pleased. This was the real David—faithful, unselfish, worshipful, the psalmist, the prophet, the beloved. With such actions he bound men's hearts to him with unbreakable cords. This was the man after God's own heart, the forerunner of Israel's everlasting King.

What is the lesson for us? Are we of those who are so dull and proper that we do not stir without written orders? Can we imagine David writing out an order or summoning the three to say, "Go to Bethlehem and bring me some of my own village water"? His orders could be definite enough when occasion demanded, but there was a wide realm where his desire and need made orders superfluous. So with David's Lord; His general marching orders are clear, but we shall miss the glory of His highest service if we fail to read His heart.

No one told Mary to bring her spikenard. No one summoned the tenth healed leper and commanded him to fall on his face at his Healer's feet. No one ordered Joseph to give up his own new tomb, or Nicodemus to bring his weight of spices.

It is our responsibility to know our Lord's desire for us. Who would not preach to multitudes and see them yielding to the Saviour's claims? Who would not be entrusted with wealth to give to meet some of the needs of the world? But the question is: "What is His design for me?" The three seized upon David's thirsty sigh and risked all.

We are inclined to complain that it is hard to know the Lord's desire for us. It is not easy, but it is simple. The three were near enough to David to hear him express his longing; if we are occupying the place of nearness, we shall not mistake the echo of our own wills for His voice.

When David poured out his drink offering as an act of worship, he could not know that he was foreshowing his Lord, who, becoming Great High Priest, would daily perform such a service for His worshipping ones as He takes their humble gifts, praise, service, money, time, body, soul, spirit. Mean in themselves, they are of infinite worth when related to His sacrifice, for they are accepted as He Himself is accepted, precious in His priceless worth, glorious in the glory of His enthroned Person.

But everything depends on that breaking through with irresistible resolve. We are unnecessarily straitened in ourselves and we submit tamely, fearing the enemy when we should be breaking through his ranks with audacious faith.

This is what the friends of the palsied man did to reach the Lord Jesus: they broke through, using ingenuity and strength. This is what the Lord Jesus did: He broke through the conventions of heaven and earth that He might be *"found in fashion as a Man"* and become *"obedient unto death."* This is what the apostles did when they broke through the forbidding customs of Judaism. This is what the Reformers did when they broke through the armies of Rome and gave us the Scriptures. This is what the early missionaries did when they broke through the resistance of a disobedient Church. This is what men such as Müller did when they broke through the forces of formalism.

This is what we want our young men to do who have not yet made their calling and election sure. We have not yet heard their testimony in the open air. We listen in vain for their voices giving fresh thanks at the Table of Remembrance. We miss them at the prayer meeting and we fear they have not yet made the Scriptures their intensive study.

The ranks of the careless and godless have never felt the shock of their approach, because they have not yet broken through their reserve, respectability, preoccupation; they have no scars to show—

not yet, at least—but it is not too late to win the mastery.

May these nameless three, and the pre-eminent One of Bethlehem put such to honest shame, that soon the shock of their assault shall be felt in heaven and earth and hell.

—A. C. Rose, July-August 1997, pp. 6-7

26. Heaven Now or Later?

 he was a friendly, helpful person, middle-aged, and worked in a local toy store in the junior department. She was usually bright and cheerful, a nice lady. We made frequent visits to her department picking up gifts, and we got to know her. I had frequent opportunities to leave a gospel tract or to have a talk to her about the Lord and her need of salvation. Her worldly interests, however, seemed more important and she showed little concern.

One Friday about closing time, I had to pick up a gift for one of the children, and as I was going down the stairs to where this lady worked, she looked up and saw me coming. "Oh, Mr. Nicholson, please don't preach to me tonight. I've had a bad week and a very rough day." I assured her I wasn't there to 'preach' to her. I just wanted a little gift.

"Anyway," she went on, "I've made a decision."

"And what is that?" I queried with interest.

"I've decided that this life is all the hell I'm ever going to have." The forcefulness—almost anger—of her words, took me aback for a moment.

"Well," I replied, "I won't preach to you, but I do want to correct your serious mistake."

Defensively now, she asked, "What mistake?"

"If you die without ever having received the Lord Jesus as your Saviour, this life is all the *heaven* you're going to have, so you better enjoy it!"

She didn't want to talk, and I left the store. Soon after, the store moved, and I have never again seen that lady.

This encounter brought very forcefully to me the desperate condition of the lost in this desert world, where its wanderers are deceived by the visions of glittering oases, only to discover when they reach out to touch them they are nothing but mirages of empty promise, broken cisterns, faded beauty. They turn up the volume of their music so they will not need to hear the sob of the sorrowing, the cry of the suffering, the wail of the dying all around them, and the persistent voice of their own consciences.

In 2 Kings 6–7, we have a picture of this emptiness. Samaria was being besieged. The situation was desperate. Women were boiling their own babies and eating them! How shocking, yet what a picture this is of the desperate emptiness of the lost. Those despairing mothers cried out to the king for help, but there was none—nothing but the king's mourning that only added to their grief.

But there is a God of mercy, full of tender compassion. Through His servant Elisha, He sent word that within twenty-four hours the city would have an abundance of the finest food. He had His servants waiting to work out His will. What unlikely servants!

Who would those servants be that would deliver the city from the mighty Syrians? Captains of the host? Men of valor? No, just four desperate lepers ready to die. These four men were going to die somehow, either by starvation, or by their disease. So they thought they would go out to the Syrians, throw themselves on their mercy, and see what happened.

In the meantime, the Lord had terrified the Syrians with the noise of a great army. They fled and left everything behind—food, clothes, silver and gold. This is what the four lepers found—an empty camp—with everything! In their exhilaration, they ran from tent to tent, eating and plundering until suddenly they came to their senses and remembered their own people starving back in Samaria.

Which one of the men said it we are not told, but, one of them, the rest concurring, made a statement that should sound out in our day like a trumpet call. It should alarm us that our neighbors, friends, schoolmates, and loved ones are perishing in a desert world *"where no water is."* They are trying with so much effort, time, and money, to turn it into some kind of a paradise. Multitudes try to get a piece of the golden calf (with just a little "luck" at the lottery). But *"time happeneth to all men"* and only a lost eternity lies before them.

They said: *"We do not well: this day is a day of good tidings, and we hold our peace: if we tarry till the morning light, some mischief will come upon us: now therefore come, that we may go and tell..."* (2 Ki. 7:9).

We would do well if we followed the example of those four leprous men. They recognized their obligation to the perishing souls nearby. They recognized the time of opportunity was brief: *"this day."* They recognized their duty was obvious and simple: *"Go and tell"* the *"glad tidings."* So they did, and the incredulous people were saved through the goodness of God and the faithfulness of those *"four leprous men."* They did it, and so can you.

> *Rescue the perishing! Care for the dying,*
> *Snatch them in pity from sin and the grave;*
> *Weep o'er the erring ones, lift up the fallen,*
> *Tell them of Jesus, the mighty to save.*
> —Fanny Crosby

—*J. Boyd Nicholson, Editorial, May-June 1999, p. 3*

27. JOSEPH

f all the Old Testament characters, Joseph is one of the most beautiful pictures of the Lord Jesus. There are numerous parallels between the life of Joseph and the life of the Lord Jesus. Although Joseph partook of the sin nature, there is no record of failure in his life. This adds to the value of the picture in relation to the Lord Jesus, who Himself only was sinless and impeccable. Therefore we may learn much concerning the Person and work of Christ as we study Joseph.

We see Joseph as the son of the father, the suffering servant, the sovereign of Egypt, the succourer of his brethren, and the sequel of faith.

OVERVIEW OF HIS LIFE

Christologically: It has been reckoned by some scholars that there are over one hundred parallels between the life of Joseph and the life of Christ. Some of the more obvious are listed below.

JOSEPH	CHRIST
Object of the father's love & pleasure	Mt. 3:17; Mk. 1:11; Lk. 3:22
Obedient to the father's will	Heb. 10:9; Jn. 8:29
Rejected by his brethren	Jn. 1:10-11
Misunderstood by his brethren	Mt. 26:55; Mk. 14:58; Lk. 6:2-3
Sold by his brethren	Mt. 26:15
Suffered at the hands of the Gentiles	Mt. 26; Mk. 14&15; Lk. 23 & 24
Exalted to the throne	Phil. 2:9-11; Eph. 1:20-23

Historically: The experiences of Joseph from his father's house to the place where he reached the throne—by way of the sufferings of the pit and the prison—have had their accurate fulfillment in the life, death, and resurrection of Christ, and His exaltation to God's right hand. Like Joseph, the suffering of the Lord Jesus is now past, and He has entered into glory.

In the present age: When Joseph was in exile from his brethren, he took a bride to himself from among the Gentiles. So it is concerning Christ. Israel is now, in this Church age, set aside nationally, and the Lord is now exalted. During this time, the Lord Jesus is calling out a people, both Jew and Gentile, to form the Church of God. This is the Bride, who will share His throne and His love for all eternity.

Prophetically: Just as much of the life of Joseph has found its counterpart in the life of Christ, there remains much that has yet to be fulfilled in relation to the repentance of His people, the subsequent reconciliation that will take place, and their links with Him on the Throne.

The famine in Canaan drove Israel and his family into the arms of Joseph. So shall it be in the future day. The horrors of tribulation "the great one" will drive that unbelieving nation back to God. Then they will seek His delivering power when all others will have turned their backs on them.

Joseph's brethren were tested as to the reality of their repentance by the things that Joseph brought upon them. He tested them in the matter of the returned silver, then in the matter of the cup found in Benjamin's sack. It is evident that the years had softened those brothers' hearts, the hearts that had been shut up against the cries of Joseph when they put him in the pit, then sold him. Now they pled for Benjamin, and offered to take his place.

Israel will be brought to a place of repentance in a day to come as the crushing events of great tribulation take hold on them. Eventually, Joseph had enough evidence to confirm the reality of their repentance. Then he made himself known to them, saying, *"I am Joseph."* The chapters describing the recognition of Joseph, the fear and trembling of his brethren, and his super-abounding love must surely be among the most touching chapters in the Bible.

When the Tribulation has brought Israel to the point of annihilation at the hands of her enemies, it is then that her Messiah will appear in power and glory (Isa. 59), and all the armies of heaven with Him. Israel will see their Messiah, and to their amazement, He will have wounds in His hands!

Quickly they will recognize that the One whom they crucified in shame outside the city wall was indeed their Messiah, and they will tremble. Zechariah 13–14 outlines the events that will unfold for Israel then. Deep mourning will overtake that nation when they realize that they crucified their own Messiah. Yet even in such days of grief, there will be a fountain opened for sin and uncleanness, and the nation will be forgiven.

Thereafter, the Christ will assume His place on the throne of David, and as Messiah, He will reign for a thousand years—the Millennium described in Revelation 20.

THE SOVEREIGN PURPOSE OF GOD

Looking at the life of Joseph from a purely natural point of view, we would be inclined to think that his life was a series of uncontrolled disasters, which by some stroke of fate made a dramatic turnaround at the end. There were many who had done him ill through the years, and it would have been natural for him to seek redress, and to punish those who had hated him, sold him, and slandered him. But we find that when Joseph reached the throne, he was full of forgiveness and displayed his beneficence even to those who had made his life such a misery over the years.

How was this possible? Joseph had a perspective on life that went beyond the happenings and hurts that he had endured along the way. He had a grasp of the fact that life, with all of its ups and downs, its trials and tribulations, was controlled by a sovereign God, and Joseph could say, *"Ye thought evil against me; but God meant it unto good"* (Gen. 50:20).

Oh, that we all today could view the happenings of life from this aspect! How we would be saved from petty criticisms and personal touchiness to every little hurt received, perceived or otherwise.

If we held this high view of life, even major events, that at the time seemed catastrophic and changed the course of our lives, would be seen in the softer, kinder light of the sovereignty of God.

Do we believe that a sovereign God is at work in and over our lives? Or do we think like the ungodly, that we are at the mercy of events and people that cross our path? We would find much peace in our hearts if we had the confidence that *"all things work together for good to them that love God."*

Even in his darkest hours, when Joseph was in the prison house of Pharaoh, we read that *"the Lord was with Joseph."* When his brethren eventually came to know him, they were filled with fear. Joseph quietly set their fears aside by bringing them into the good of his view of life and its circumstances. He reminded them of his conviction that *"God meant it for good to save many people alive this day."* God can make even the wrath of His enemies to praise Him.

Think of Paul, under similar circumstances to Joseph—bound and in prison. He writes to the Philippians, telling them that the fact of his imprisonment has worked out for the good, and *"fallen out rather unto the furtherance of the gospel."*

Even in connection with the death of the Saviour at Calvary, Peter on the day of Pentecost, speaking concerning the death of Christ, reminds Israel of the sovereign ways of God, even of such an event: *"Him being delivered by the determinate counsel and foreknowledge of God…"*

May God grant us that peace of mind, that ambience of spirit, that attitude of forgiveness, and that love that embraces even our enemies and those who have sought to harm and discredit us, by holding fast to the truth of the sovereign purposes of God being worked out in our lives.

—W. H. Burnett, May-June 1997, pp. 16-17

efore the cross, the Lord Jesus gathered His beloved few around Him in that upper room. Full well He knew what lay before Him, and what sorrow would soon befall His own. They needed words to help them now. So He taught them some vital lessons before He would leave them.

He thought of the dark night of sorrow they would enter, of the tears they would shed and their lamenting grief, and He wanted to prepare them: *"The world shall rejoice; and ye shall be sorrowful"* (Jn. 16:20).

"But"—here is the rainbow after the rain, the sunrise after the long night—*"But your sorrow shall be turned into joy."* Not replaced by joy, their sorrow would itself be transfigured into joy. The cause of their sorrow would become the source of their joy.

They may have recalled David's assuring song in the sunshine: *"Weeping may endure for a night, but joy cometh in the morning"* (Ps. 30:5). An old translation puts it, "Weeping comes as a traveller in the night to tarry, but joy comes in the morning to abide."

It is this certain hope that has sustained the saints through the ages in their dark nights of weeping. Ancient Job, in the furnace of affliction, said, *"But He knoweth the way that I take: when He hath tried me, I shall come forth as gold"* (Job 23:10).

We are not pawns in the hand of some distant deity for his amusement. We are not feathers blown by the fickle winds of fate, chemical coincidences, genetic accidents. No indeed! God's people are a work in His hand, *"created for His glory"* (Isa. 43:7).

Jeremiah went down to the potter's house and saw *"the vessel that he made of clay was marred in the hand of the potter: so he made it again another vessel, as seemed good to the potter to make it"* (Jer. 18:4).

The whole idea of God's purpose of present grace and future glory came to me forcibly recently while sitting reading in the sunroom at home. Hanging in the window there is a small solid glass ball. When the sun is not shining on it, it is just a transparent orb, hardly ever noticed. But when the sun strikes it, suddenly it seems to come alive with light. The whole room is blessed with the radiance of the rainbow it reflects.

You see, at some time an expert craftsman ground all around the surface of that glass ball, 118 facets. Every facet radiates the glory of the sunlight into my room. Yet I have never heard anyone say, "My, what a beautiful piece of glass," but often I have heard them marvel at the colors of the rainbow splashing my room with beauty.

Down here in the valley of weeping, day by day, the loving, gracious Holy Spirit with divine skill is working on the lives of the saints by all the grinding circumstances of life, meticulously controlling and cutting facet after facet into the life, until we feel we can stand no more and cry out for help and relief.

Then comes the morning! A sunrise that has no sunset, and the glory of the Lord will burst upon His people. Then all those facets, wrought together, uniquely and individually into each life by the patient Holy Spirit, will then blaze with light, reflecting first to the heart of the Father and then to the gaze of wondering angels, the glories and beauties of our beloved Lord. The Father will be satisfied, the Lord Jesus will be magnified, the saints will be glorified, and the angels will be mystified.

Those angels will not say, "My, what beautiful Christians they turned out to be," but rather, "What a glorious Lord, to make such beautiful repositories of His radiance out of such unlovely stuff." We shall be *"to the praise of His glory"* (Eph. 1:12).

The Father, who gave up His beloved Son, the One who awakened the sword of inflexible justice and drew it from its blazing scabbard to smite the Good Shepherd, will be able to say on that great day of the gathering and the glory, "It was worth it all," and He shall be satisfied.

The Lord Jesus, who left His heavenly home and came to this poor, pathetic planet to seek and to save that which was lost, to be rejected and despised by His creatures, will look at last upon that shining company arrayed before Him in glistering glory, the fruit of His travail, and He will be able to say, "It was worth it all," and He shall be satisfied.

In breathless wonder, we, His redeemed, will realize in a moment that we have awakened in a blaze of glory, forever to bear His likeness and we shall be able to say, "Satisfied, Lord Jesus...with Thy likeness."

> *And God has fixed the happy day,*
> *When the last tear shall dim our eyes,*
> *When He will wipe those tears away,*
> *And fill our hearts with glad surprise;*
> *To hear His voice, and see His face,*
> *And know the fullness of His grace.*
> —Joseph Swain

—J. Boyd Nicholson, Editorial, January-February 1998, p. 3

29. THE SOWER AND THE SEED (MK. 4:14)

 olumbus, it is said, carried the seeds of flowers and scattered them wherever his vessel anchored. This simple act of the explorer may have seemed insignificant to his associates, but it left for Columbus a perpetual monument in the beautiful flowers of Spain, blooming hundreds of years after his death in distant lands.

Seed has the capacity to reproduce itself and multiply from year to year, and so the reward to the sower abides perpetually. The labor of the builder may crumble and perish, but the sower of good seed has an everlasting compensation.

IT IS SOWING, NOT SAVING

No work is more noble or fraught with more blessed possibilities than the work of sowing the seed of the gospel. If you prayerfully scatter gospel tracts and preach Christ to others by lip and deed you will leave behind you, or carry with you, a more glorious reward than those who make millions or shape the destiny of nations. It is what you sow, not what you save, that will leave the flowers of the Good Land behind you to bless your memory.

IT IS DYING, NOT SPARING

The Lord Jesus called Himself a sower. He left no buildings or institutions behind Him to perpetuate His name. He did not organize His disciples into a fraternity. He merely sowed. He sowed the Word of God in the hearts of men and sowed Himself in the earth. *"Except a corn of wheat fall into the ground and die, it abideth alone: but if it die, it bringeth forth much fruit."* He went forth in sorrow, *"bearing precious seed."* He wept, He sighed, He was weary with His journey. It was His sowing time. But what a harvest from that sowing! There was a *"handful of corn in the earth"* when the Lord laid in the sepulcher of Joseph of Arimathea but even now the fruit of it begins to *"shake like Lebanon."*

IT IS NOT RESTING BUT REAPING

Why is Paul, the beaten, imprisoned servant of Jesus Christ, better known than the rulers of the empires of his day? Because he sowed. Paul tramped the roads of Asia and Europe sowing, like his Master, the Word of God, the glad tidings of the gospel to every creature under heaven. They put chains on his hands but they could not bind the Word of God.

They wrote his name on the criminal roll in Jerusalem, in Philippi, and in Rome, but the man whose gray head was severed from his body for the sake of Christ has left a more enduring monument to his memory than those who rode in triumph and slept in palaces. The love of the Thessalonians, the sacrificial devotedness of the Philippians, the tears and embraces at Ephesus, all told of the fertile soil the good seed of the gospel had found.

They could kill the apostle at Rome but he continued to live in the hearts of those who were led to Christ through his testimony. We will search in vain for the name of Paul in the records of his day, but the earth is full of the fruit of the seed that he sowed.

WHAT TO SOW

"The sower soweth the Word" (Mk. 4:14). That Word is *"living and powerful."* The gospel is *"the power of God unto salvation to every one that believeth."* Sow the glad tidings of salvation with confidence; it is invincible and indestructible.

WHEN TO SOW

"In the morning sow thy seed, and in the evening withhold not thine hand" (Eccl. 11:6). In the morning when the heart is light and the prospect inviting; in the evening when the foot is weary and the sky overcast. In the morning of youth when the zeal of first love burns brightly; in the evening of age when the day is almost done. When the heart is willing, it is never too early and never too late to sow.

WHERE TO SOW

"Blessed are ye that sow beside all waters" (Isa. 32:20). Rivers flow in all lands; there are waters in China as well as in America. The people beside all waters need the gospel. *"The bread of life"* cast upon the waters in distant lands may be found in the glory by the sower *"after many days."*

There are little streams in the countryside as well as broad rivers flowing to the ocean. Who can tell where the seed will grow. *"Beside all waters,"* said the prophet. We should sow the gospel everywhere. In the barber shop, in the dentist's chair, over the grocery counter, drop the gospel seed anywhere. Some will find fertile soil. Let us go home to heaven sowing.

HOW TO SOW

"He which soweth bountifully shall reap also bountifully" (2 Cor. 9:6). A wise man will be sparing in his spending rather than in his sowing. One way to sow bountifully is to *"minister seed to the sower."* There are those who sow in every nation under heaven. God has His witnesses everywhere. Those who have gone forth *"for His name's sake...taking nothing of the Gentiles,"* deserve our sympathy and help. They are sowers. If we cannot sow there ourselves, let us supply the seed to those who do. The Lord said of the gifts of the Corinthians, *"He that ministereth seed to the sower both minister bread for your food, and multiply your seed sown, and increase the fruits of your righteousness."*

IT IS SOWING, NOT BURYING

If you would *"reap in joy,"* dear fellow believer, you must sow. Sow by your tongue and your testimony; sow by your gifts and your labor. If you bury a talent in the earth, you will be an eternal loser. Sow in faith till your body is sown in hope or till hope is crowned with glory at the coming of our Lord. Perhaps the measure of our faith is the measure in which we sow.

COMPENSATIONS

"Now what will you give this gentleman for saving your life?" said a fond mother to her little daughter as she stood, all prim and nice again in her dry clothes, before strong John Ellerthorpe. She looked at the manly sailor who had pulled her from the water, then held up her little chin and out of a full heart said, "A kiss."

John Ellerthorpe, in relating the incident, said, "I felt myself well paid for the trouble, and had a deeper feeling of joy and satisfaction when that grateful child kissed me, than I did when the town folk presented me with a reward."

IT IS HOPING, NOT HOARDING

"What is our hope, or joy, or crown of rejoicing?" wrote the apostle to the Thessalonian Christians. He added, *"Are not even ye in the presence of our Lord Jesus Christ at His coming? For ye are our glory and joy."* To be an instrument in the salvation of precious souls is a joy that only those who have tasted it can know.

To see happy saints in the presence of the Lord at His coming, for whom *you* labored and travailed, and to whom *you* brought the word of life, will be a source of unspeakable joy. To be a soul winner has its compensation now. The miser may have his wealth and the covetous man his gain, but give me the joy of affectionate appreciation in the hearts of those blessed through my sowing.

IT IS REJOICING AND REAPING

The richest joy of all will be the harvest joy. Then sower and reaper will rejoice together. *"He that reapeth receiveth wages and gathereth fruit unto life eternal, that both he that soweth and he that reapeth may rejoice together."* To share in the honors and gladness of that day will more than compensate for any sorrow or loss now. Let us sow now in this springtime, lest like the sluggard at harvest time there be nothing but thorns and briars on our fields.

THE SOWER AND THE SEED

Sowing the seed by the daylight fair,
Sowing the seed by the noonday glare,
Sowing the seed in the fading light,
Sowing the seed in the solemn night
Oh, what shall the harvest be?

Sowing the seed with an aching heart,
Sowing the seed while the teardrops start,
Sowing in hope till the reapers come
Gladly to gather the harvest home:
Oh what shall the harvest be?

(Mrs. Emily Sullivan Oakley)

—Leonard Sheldrake, November-December 1999, pp. 14-15

30. Aunt Elsie and the Gederites

ver the olive trees and the sycamore trees that were in the low plains was Baal-hanan the Gederite: and over the cellars of oil was Joash" (1 Chron. 27:28).

She was a real caricature: any artist would have delighted to pull out a pencil and sketch her. Little and old—well, she was in her 80's—rather a long nose and a somewhat pointed chin. She wore an old oatmeal gray coat, sometimes buttoned in the right button hole and sometimes not. On her head was a black felt hat, pressed on at a different angle each night. But she had the most electric blue eyes, with a sparkle that indicated that behind the old frame and beneath the fading locks was a very active mind.

It was the dead of Canadian winter and there was a series of gospel meetings being held nightly. She lived alone, so we picked her up in the car and took her along to the meetings. She didn't miss one night in five weeks.

Night by night after the meeting, this old soldier would greet the preacher at the door with a rather succinct assessment of the message. "Well," she might say one night, "You had a hard time preaching up there tonight, didn't you?" Indeed, it was one of those nights when there seemed to be no liberty at all to preach, fumbling through the message, forgetting, misquoting–a distressing thing for a preacher.

"Yes, Aunt Elsie," the preacher replied, "I was really struggling tonight."

The old lady nodded, "Well, I'm praying for you."

"Thank you, sister, I need it."

On another night, it would be different, the strong handshake at the door and the "appraisal." "Well, God gave help in preaching the old gospel tonight brother."

"Yes, thank the Lord, there was help and liberty in the message tonight," said the preacher.

Fastening those eyes on him, she'd reply, "I'm praying for you."

It was not clear whether that was to be a prayer for blessing or for humbling, lest the preacher glory in himself or his preaching.

Then one night, a terrifying thing for a preacher took place. Sitting at the front just about to climb the platform to speak, the preacher was going over in his mind the message he had prepared. The last hymn before he should rise was coming to a close, when suddenly, it was as though the Lord spoke in his heart and said, "That is not the message for tonight!" What a shock, in such a moment. In a minute he would have to get up and preach—what? Crying in his heart to the Lord for help, suddenly, and very forcibly, there came to mind an obscure Old Testament scripture. The Lord helped the preacher quickly locate the scripture, the hymn ended, and with his finger in the text he climbed the platform, opened the Bible, and with trembling began to preach the gospel from that obscure text. God blessed the message in a wonderful way and souls professed faith in Christ that night.

The preacher stood at the door but he was looking for the little black hat making its way down the aisle. What was the saintly old prayer warrior going to say to him tonight?

At last there she was. She took hold of the preacher's hand, held onto it, and fastened those twinkling eyes on him for a long minute. "Well, I prayed for you today—that you would preach from that very text tonight!"

It is doubtful if anyone ever went to that old soul to thank her for praying for the needy preacher, but if there are to be rewards for the work accomplished in those meetings, where do you think they will go? To the man on the pulpit or the old prayer warrior doing business for God and the souls of men in the sanctuary, wrestling in heavenly places to pull down the anointing of God on the public testimony?

Remember Baal-hanan the Gederite? Or Joash of the oil cellars? Not likely. Few ever remember them. Why not? Because as far as we can tell, those men never said a word in any of the public service of God. They were commissioned by the king to ensure that there would always be an adequate inventory of oil for the anointing of the holy vessels.

Baal-hanan labored in *"the low plains"* and Joash in *"the cellars."* Men out of sight, yet whose hidden ministry was absolutely essential for all the service of the sanctuary. Indeed, without their hidden labors there would be no public service at all.

We have learned to thank God for the saints of the sanctuary. Without this, all our preaching would be but a superfluity of words, falling to the ground. Those men of the oil were unknown, unseen, unheralded, but the king knew they were there; he had commissioned them, and he would reward them.

Well, Aunt Elsie was little known down here, laboring in *"the low plains"* and in *"the cellars"*—but she was well known in the sanctuary. The Lord knew she was there. He had commissioned her and He will reward her.

Thank God for the servants of the sanctuary.

—J. Boyd Nicholson, Editorial, May-June 2000, p. 3

31. THE QUESTION AT THE BUS STOP

ack in the days of rationing in World War II, the use of small plastic coins was in vogue in the U.S. These were called "mills" and had to be given with each purchase. They were made of red plastic and their actual value was a minute fraction of a cent.

One day, while standing at a bus stop, a man dropped one of these red mills and it rolled through the crowd to my feet. I bent over and retrieved it and fought my way through the people until I reached the man who had dropped it and handed it to him. He gazed at me in mild wonderment and said, "Thanks for a tenth of a cent!"

I replied, "You are entirely welcome." Then I said to him, "You don't meet many people who would bother to thank you for something of such inconsequential value. You belong to a rare breed."

The man laughed easily. "Whatever my faults are, and they are many, ingratitude is not one of them. There are so many unthankful people in the world. That's what is wrong with it. But me, well, I have always made it a point to be thankful for anything anyone has ever done for me, no matter how small it may be. That is why I thanked you for that token."

"I'm pleased to meet a person like you. You don't meet many thankful people."

"Well, you're looking at one now!"

"If you are so careful to render thanks for the seemingly worthless, you would undoubtedly be thankful for even greater things."

"For example?" he queried.

I replied, "Did you ever hear of the Lord Jesus Christ?"

"Yes. Who hasn't?"

"Well," I said watching the bus approach, "you know He died on the cross for the sins of this world and He died for mine. I never knew that until a few years ago and I trusted Him as my Saviour. I thanked Him for dying for me. Now, a man like yourself who would thank a person for a fraction of a cent has certainly thanked God for giving His Son to die for his sins so he could go to heaven. Tell me, when did you thank Him for dying for you?"

A tinge of red crept into the man's cheek. Dropping his eyes, he said in an almost inaudible voice, "I can't say that I have ever done that."

The bus drew up and the door opened; people crowded in. "Mister," said I, "how are you going to face God some day when the books are opened and the record says you thanked me for a tenth of a cent but you never thanked Him for giving His Son to die for you?"

The man paused for a split second and gave me an inscrutable look, then disappeared into the bus.

What he ever did about it I don't know, but right now I'm wondering about you, the reader. Have you ever thanked Him for dying on the cross for your sins? How will your record read when you stand before Him? Will you be numbered among that vast multitude of whom it was written, *"Neither were thankful"*?

—Leonard Lindsted, March-April 2000, p. 18

32. Tears—in Heaven! (Rev. 5)

The pages of human history and the pillows of aching humanity have been stained with tears from the earliest days. Something has gone wrong! Surely this was not the way it was supposed to be! God had made earth a paradise for His creatures. Adam and his consort were to *"have dominion"* over the earth and over nature.

What pure delight must have filled the early days of our first parents. What must it have been each morning to be awakened by the rising sun as it poured its pure light on the verdant hills, transforming the drops of morning dew into liquid diamonds? The atmosphere, redolent with the fragrance of fruit and flowers would make each breath an exhilarating delight. The serenade of the songbird would fill their ears with harmony and their hearts with joy. Then, as each day progressed, they would anticipate with ecstacy their highest blessing, the evening walk with God their loving Creator.

But there was an enemy!

Sin invaded the kingdom and dethroned its king. Adam abdicated his dominion to Satan. His crown in the dust, he and his consort went into exile, expelled from the life and fellowship of God.

That is what has gone wrong and we all know it, because we are all affected by it: *"Wherefore, as by one man sin entered into the world, and death by sin; and so death passed upon all men, for that all have sinned."* We hear it in the groan of the sufferer, the wail of the dying, and see it in the bitter tears of the sorrowing.

Can it ever be put right? Can anyone invade this realm and with mighty power wrest the kingdom back from the evil usurper? Is there one who is worthy and able to recover the title deeds of the earth and set up a new order where mercy and truth shall meet, and righteousness and peace shall kiss?

That was the question the mighty angel asked in heaven where John had been caught up. He had just heard the Lord's worthiness declared and the purpose of creation expressed, *"Thou hast created all things, and for Thy pleasure they are and were created."* This

111

revealed that it was not just mankind that suffered loss, but the Lord who had created it all.

Before John's vision the Mighty Occupant of the throne sat holding out the sealed scroll, the title deeds of the inheritance forfeited by sin, to any who could take it and open the seals, thereby claiming the inheritance. Down through the centuries, many have tried to claim that right. The Pharaohs of Egypt, the kings of Babylon, the Caesars of Rome, the emperors of Europe, but none was worthy enough, and none was mighty enough. Now the call goes out from heaven, *"Who is worthy to open the book, and to loose the seals thereof?"* Silence! No mighty angel stepped forward to take up the challenge, none of the spirits of just men made perfect in glory made a move, not Moses, not Elijah, not Paul, not any! *"No one...was able..."*

Such a sight the angels had never beheld: tears—in heaven! Why did John weep much? Being *"in the Spirit,"* John would know the implications if no one was found worthy. All the promises of a mighty Deliverer, all the declarations of the prophets, the long hope of *"the redemption of the purchased possession"* must fall to the ground and the elect who had suffered unjustly and *"which cry day and night"* to God would never be avenged.

And Israel—what about the covenant with Abraham, the promises? A seed, a land, a glorious temple, a kingdom, the head of the nations—is it all a deception? The faithfulness of God—is it all a delusion? The sobbing of the disciple whom Jesus loved, as he *"wept much"* was the only sound before the throne.

O thank God! That is not the end of the story! The silence is broken; an elder speaks, *"Weep not; behold the Lion of the tribe of Judah..."* John lifts his tearstained face. *"...the Root of David, hath prevailed to open the book, and to loose the seals thereof."*

Ah! that is the answer; a Mighty Monarch clothed with power and majesty to inflict terror upon His enemies. But what did John see? *"A lamb as it had been slain."* Wonder not, the Lamb is omnipotent, having *"seven horns;"* omniscient, having *"seven eyes;"* omnipresent *"into all the earth"* and it is by His sacrificial death. Yet now He is a living Lamb, still bearing in His person the marks of His anguish. He is worthy to take the book.

As a Lion, He will judge and make war and enforce the rule of His throne, but it is from the wrath of the Lamb the wicked will seek to flee.

Now it is John who is silent. His tears are dried, his soul amazed, his spirit overwhelmed as the new song of heaven rolls over him like the waves of the sea. The universal choirs resound to fill the infinities of space, *"Worthy is the Lamb..."* We, the redeemed of the Lord, join the living creatures with relief to say *"Amen"* and bow with the elders to *"Him that liveth for ever and ever"* in adoring worship.

—*J. Boyd Nicholson, Editorial, July-August 1998, p. 3*

33. REUBEN THE FALLEN PATRIARCH

he Lord, through Isaac, confirmed the Abrahamic Covenant to Jacob. He was warned not to take a wife of the daughters of Canaan. Isaac suggests that he go to the home of his uncle Laban and take one of his daughters for a wife. When Jacob arrived there, Laban wanted Jacob to stay and care for his flocks. *"What will be your wages?"* asks Laban. Now Laban had two daughters, Leah and Rachel. They were both beautiful girls, but Jacob loved Rachel. *"I will serve seven years for your youngest daughter,"* Jacob vows.

At the end of the seven years, the wedding feast was held. The seven years had passed quickly because of his love for Rachel. What a wonderful picture of our service for the Lord! Our work for Him should never be tedious.

However, the day after the wedding was consummated, Jacob discovered that Laban had tricked him. He was married to Leah and not Rachel. Laban also gave Rachel to Jacob for his wife, but he would have to serve seven more years without pay. Jacob was reaping the wages of the deceit he had sown.

With two wives, Jacob obviously wanted to have children. We read that Jacob loved Rachel more than Leah. However, the Lord hindered Rachel from bearing. But Leah began to have children. Her first child was a son. She named him Reuben, which means *"See, a son."* She was sure Jacob's love for her would increase since she had given him a son.

Eleven other sons were born to the two wives and their handmaids. No doubt Leah hoped Reuben would grow to be a great shepherd and a strong warrior, and Jacob's attitude would change towards her. But Jacob's first love was still with Rachel.

Things were not all sunshine and roses in the household. There were jealousies between the two women. An event recorded in Genesis 30 highlights this. Reuben found mandrakes in the field and brought them to his mother. It was some sort of a fruit that was supposed to impart fertility. Rachel asked for the mandrakes. Leah had four boys and Rachel desperately wanted a child. Possibly Leah was out of favor as a wife at this time. So Rachel promised Leah that she could live as a wife with Jacob in exchange for the mandrakes. This resulted in Leah bearing two more sons.

We are not told how old Reuben was at this time, but I wonder if he observed how the people of God will sometime resort to sinful means to get their way instead of trusting Him for the outcome. Could this ever be true of us?

The Bible always speaks plainly. Sins are not glossed over. The record of Reuben's sin is given in Genesis 35:22 and 1 Chronicles 5:1-2. All of the hopes of blossoming youth were crushed by one indiscreet act, causing this eldest son of Jacob to lose his birthright. Not only Reuben but all his descendants would suffer from this one deed. We little realize what consequences can occur when we engage in what we think is a "minor sin." God sees every sin as serious. When the children of Israel entered the land more than 400 years later, the land was divided, with the sons of Joseph getting the double birthright portion instead of the children of Reuben.

As the brothers became adults, a fierce rivalry arose between Joseph and his brethren. We read how the brothers were in the field, tending their flocks. Jacob sent Joseph to see how his brothers were doing. Joseph arrived, wearing his coat of special distinction. How they hated him and were ready to kill him! But it was Reuben who suggested they not kill him but cast him into a pit nearby.

Some time later, the other brothers sold Joseph to a passing band of Ishmaelites. Reuben had not taken part in this transaction; he was probably away for a time. He was upset when he returned and discovered Joseph was gone. In fact he reminded his brothers of this when they stood before the ruler of Egypt—Joseph in disguise.

At the end of Jacob's life, we are given an unusual scene in Genesis 49. Jacob and all his family were living in Egypt, having been brought there by Joseph. All the sons are gathered around the deathbed of Jacob and he begins to tell them what would occur in the last days. This prophecy foretold the history of the Jewish race as well as of each tribe.

Of Reuben he says, *"Thou art my firstborn, my might, and the beginning of my strength, the excellency of dignity, and the excel-*

lency of power." No doubt he expected great things from his first-born son. However, Jacob continues, *"[Thou art] unstable as water, and shall not excel"* (Gen. 49:3-4). This was fulfilled as the Israelites returned to the Promised Land. The tribe of Reuben settled on the wilderness side of the Jordan River.

From this tribe came no judge, no king, and no prophet. Yet, how wonderful, our God is a forgiving God. When Ezekiel saw the events that are to take place during the Millennial age, he learned that the land will be equally divided among the tribes of Israel, and Reuben is included. One of the gates of the heavenly city is named for Reuben (Ezek. 48:31). The Jewish evangelists listed in Revelation 7 number 144,000; and twelve thousand will come from the tribe of Reuben.

Here is a graphic lesson of God's great grace and forgiveness. *"For thou, Lord, art good, and ready to forgive, and plenteous in mercy unto all them who call upon Thee"* (Ps. 86:5).

Do we need His forgiveness? He is ready to pardon. Do we need strength in our trials? Hear the words of Moses, the intercessor: *"Let Reuben live, and not die"* (Deut. 33:6). So does our Intercessor pray for us: *"I have prayed for thee, that thy faith fail not."*

—Harold Harper, January-February 1997, pp. 4-5

34. Why Did Benaiah Bother?

he landscape today is white with newfallen snow. Blustery winds stir up a cold dusting, and sculpted drifts build across the path. The storm has passed and the sun is glistening on the layers of frosting all around. There is something fearsome about a bitter day of snowstorm, yet when it is past the sight is simply glorious.

When we look out from the warmth and security of the house when the snow is driving and the wind is blowing, it takes something very important indeed to make us buckle on our winter clothes and impel us out into that inhospitable weather.

As I saw all this snow, I thought of Benaiah the son of Jehoiada (2 Sam. 23:20-23). Now there was a man—a man's man! Fearless and courageous, the grandson of a mighty man called Kabzeel who was *"a valiant man"* with a record himself of *"many acts"* of courage. His father was a priest whose word had great authority in the kingdom. This was the influence under which Benaiah grew up. It is not surprising, then, that he also became a man of valor.

Among his many exploits for God and His people, one day he slew an enemy, a man of impressive appearance, about seven-and-a-half feet tall, whose weapon was a spear *"like a weaver's beam."* Benaiah *"plucked the spear"* out of his hand and slew him with his own weapon.

Not surprisingly, the king noticed this warrior, and he was promoted to be one of David's mighty men. In fact, he was one of an elect trio called "the three mighties." The record said *"he had the name"* among them. That was no small distinction in a battalion of men among whom were those who were *"armed with bows, and could use both the right hand and the left in hurling stones and shooting arrows out of a bow...men of war who were fit for battle...swift as roes upon the mountains."*

Then there was that day of snow, a day when there would be a strong inclination to sit by the fire with the family. Many times as our children were growing up, when a snowstorm would close everything down, and after we had dug a path out to the road, we would have the happiest times, all cozy and secure in the warmth of the house.

But not Benaiah! Oh, no! He has to get himself dressed in his warm clothes, leave his family in the house, and go out in the snow! Whatever for? Well, you see, there was that lion—in the pit! Why did he bother? The lion obviously couldn't get out of the pit. It must have been deep enough so it couldn't leap out. What was the problem? We can imagine the furious frustration of that powerful beast as it would try to get out of the pit and, slithering in the snow, fall back time and again. Actually the word for "pit" could also be "cistern," dug out to hold water. If this be so, then the lion was thrashing about in cold, slushy water.

But, we ask again, why did Benaiah even bother to get up and dress himself, get his weapon, and go out in the cold to deal with this lion? The animal wasn't going anywhere, it couldn't attack anyone, and eventually it would weaken and perish anyway.

Have you ever heard the furious roar of an angry lion close at hand? What a frightening thing! Hosea tells us, when the lion *"shall roar, then the children shall tremble."* The roar of that lion no doubt was frightening the children and distressing the people. God's people were precious to Benaiah. Often he had faced the enemy in battle to protect them; now he was not going to let them be distressed by an angry lion. Of course it meant danger, for only one was going to come out of that pit alive. It was not enough to fire off some arrows from a safe distance. He faced the beast *"in the midst"* of the pit. He was going to come to grips with the problem and deal with the cause of the people's distress.

Today many of God's people are fearful and distressed. These are the Lord's people, His redeemed, His beloved. With all their foibles and failings, to God they are *"the riches of the glory of His inheritance"* and precious to Him. Their enemy *"as a roaring lion, walketh about seeking whom he may devour."* This cruel adversary and evil slanderer would afflict believers with fear, but a Mightier than Benaiah has come, and by the weapon of His cross has bearded the lion in his den: *"the prince of this world is judged."* Still he roars to distress us, but his days are numbered and his end is sure.

May we too have a care for the Lord's people like Benaiah, even though it may mean enduring discomfort, difficulty, or even danger to protect them. Faint not in this battle, even though it may be as cold and inhospitable as *"a day of snow."*

> *Faint not, Christian! though in rage*
> *Satan doth thy soul engage;*
> *Take thee Faith's anointed shield,*
> *Bear it to the battlefield.* (James H. Evans)

—*J. Boyd Nicholson, Editorial, January-February 1999, p. 3*

35. JAMES AND FAITH (CH. 1)

James is the epistle of reality. It follows closely the sermon on the Mount. There are about thirty quotations or allusions to it in the epistle. It is written to the twelve tribes of Israel, but that does not limit it to Jewish believers any more than the Ephesian letter is limited to the Ephesians.

It was written by James, the Lord's brother according to the flesh. What a change and what a conquest of grace we see in this (Mt. 13:55-57). The epistle deals with what is practical. In chapter 1, we have practical godliness; in chapter 2, practical brotherhood; in chapter 3, practical wisdom; in chapter 4, practical holiness; and in chapter 5, practical patience.

In chapter 1, James is not teaching salvation by works (2:10), but that works are evidence of salvation, and in that all Scripture agrees. The epistle has much to say about faith as well as works. We have the trial of faith (1:3); the prayer of faith (1:6; 5:15); the riches of faith (2:5); the works of faith (2:18); and the perfecting of faith (2:22). Chapter 1 deals with the trial of faith. It is to be rejoiced in, for it produces patience, and if wisdom is needed in the trial, it can be had for the asking (v. 5). Let faith estimate things properly, as to rich and poor (vv. 10-11) and as to time and eternity (v. 12).

The following point the way to triumph in the trial, the grace of God (v. 17). Since God is that Author of all good things and is Light, He is not the Author of evil, so that while we may be tested by Him as Abraham was, we are not tempted by Him to sin. Since He is the Author of all good, He will not deny us wisdom and strength in every emergency. Oh, that when we are tried and tempted we would breathe from our hearts:

> *"I need Thee every hour, stay Thou nearby,*
> *Temptations lose their power when Thou art nigh."*
> (Annie S. Hawks)

In verse 18, we are introduced to the subject of regeneration.

Since we are born again, we have a nature that does not desire to sin. Living to its dictates empowered by the Spirit within us, we will find emancipation.

In verses 19-21, the beloved are to *put away all evil*. Let not any sin stand between you and your fellowship with God. Remember, sin snaps the link of communion. The word *"save"* in verse 21 refers to salvation from the power of sin. It is the saving of a life from dishonoring God. Part of our training for heaven is in learning to hate sin. The more we hate sin the less we will be tempted by it.

Attention to the Word of God (vv. 22-25). The Word of God is viewed in this chapter in four aspects: in regeneration (v. 18); in spiritual growth (v. 21); in correction (vv. 22-24); and in liberty (v. 25). "My freedom should be His grand control."

The continual doing of good (vv. 26-27). This positive aspect of Christianity leaves no time for the practice of sin. There are four simple principles here that govern pure godliness. There is action—*"visit"*; there is love and sympathy—*"in their affliction"*; there is appropriateness—*"the widows and fatherless"*; and there is accompanying *purity*–keeping *"unspotted from the world."*

To sum up, we have in this chapter the trial of our faith. The ways to a victorious Christian life are the recognition that God is sufficient for every emergency and will not deny us that wisdom and strength which are necessary to overcome (v. 17).

God has implanted in the believer a new nature that hates sin, and the indwelling Spirit will empower us to live according to its desires (v. 18). Known sins that are causing defeat are to be confessed and forsaken. Sin is slavery and there can be no victory where it has liberty (vv. 19-21). We must give strict attention to the Word of God. The hiding of it in our hearts will save us from sinning against God (vv. 22-25). The continual doing of good is the positive side of Christianity and leaves no time for indulgence in evil of any kind.

Let us take our Christianity seriously. Let us give Christ our best.

—Robert McClurkin, March-April 1994, p. 13

A t about 6000 feet we were crossing into Ugandan airspace, heading for Entebbe. The azure sky was punctuated with puffs of cumulus. The earth below was deep, rich green. But everything was not as peaceful as the scenery. President Idi Amin had ordered the expulsion of all Asians, limiting them to one suitcase of personal belongings. Only three days before in Zaire, we had picked up a signal on the radio that any foreign aircraft flying into Ugandan airspace would be shot down.

We couldn't raise a signal from Entebbe. The radio silence was ominous and we scanned the horizon for any speck that might suggest an approaching aircraft.

At last, only 40 miles out of Entebbe, we got a response, a curt "Permission to land."

It was a small aircraft, carrying only the pilot, a lady missionary with a sick baby, and me. The missionary was going to be met by friends from Kampala. The pilot was to pick up some missionaries' children returning to Zaire from school. I was to catch a South African Airlines flight at 10:30 that night for London.

We carried our baggage into the immigration office and fished out our papers. The measure of our welcome was soon evident on the official's face. "Don't you know," he said angrily, "that the President has forbidden any white persons to enter Uganda?" We didn't know that edict had been passed only the day before. "Get out of the country—now!" he shouted. It was more than anger. There was fear there.

"That is exactly what I want to do, on the first flight to London tonight," I replied.

"Get out the way you came in," and with that the official turned to his desk. As I tried to explain how that was impossible because the plane was to be loaded with children for Zaire, he added one more complication, "Get out of the country by 2 o'clock, or you'll be arrested." I could easily believe him as I looked around at the many armed soldiers.

From a child, I had been taught to pray. To pray for little things and for big things. We had prayed before setting out, but it was sure-ly time to pray again. As we stood there—the pilot, the missionary with her baby, and me—we looked at one another, sensing the urgency. A verse from the Bible had come to my mind. No doubt it was from God, *"Jesus Christ: who is gone into heaven, and is on the right hand of God; angels and authorities and powers being made subject unto Him"* (1 Pet. 3:21-22). So, standing there, we prayed and claimed the truth of that scripture and asked the Lord to deal with these authorities and the urgent need.

The pilot made plans to return to Zaire with his load. The mis-sionary was met by her friends and was taken off under their protec-tion. I waited, occasionally going to the gate for something that might be the answer to my dilemma. The time ticked away.

Then I saw a jet landing. As it taxied in, I could read British insignia on its side. Going to that airline counter, I inquired where that flight was going. "Non-stop to London," the agent replied.

"Wonderful! Put me on it, please." My relief was momentary.

"Sorry, sir, but that is an unscheduled flight stopping only for added fuel because of strong headwinds that have developed between here and London." Then to extinguish any candle of hope, he added, "In any case, I have the passenger list from Nairobi. Every seat is taken."

"Well," I compromised, "would you put my baggage on?" "Yes," the agent nodded, "we can do that." It was a relief to get rid of the collection of stuff I had brought out of Zaire. I felt at least more mobile now for whatever might happen.

As I watched, I saw some of the passengers alighting for a few minutes and going into the terminal through another door. I decided that perhaps this was God's provision for me, so I took up a position near the gate. When I heard the call to board and, as the passengers stepped out on to the tarmac, I moved in behind them, passing by the uniformed personnel at the gate unchallenged. I could just feel their eyes boring into the back of my neck and I waited for a shout—or worse, a shot. But none came!

Climbing up the steps, I expected a flight attendant to be there to check for a boarding pass, and I did not have one. My ticket was for the night flight on another airline. But there was no attendant at the door. Walking slowly up the aisle, I looked for that one important seat, the empty one! Every seat was full, and many small children were on the knees of adults. All were Asians, I discovered, that had already fled from Uganda to Kenya. One could feel the tension. No doubt there was much concern that they might be detained again there at Entebbe.

I went the length of the aisle without seeing a seat available. Then I passed into the first class section. A crew member came from the flight deck, and, seeing my uncertainty, asked, "Can I help you, sir?"

I hesitated. "Well, I'm looking for a seat."

"Where was your seat," he asked.

"Oh," I faltered, "I don't have a seat. I just boarded here."

"I'm sorry, but you'll have to leave the aircraft. We are not permitted to pick up passengers here. This is an unscheduled stop for fuel only." By now I had taken a quick look around. There were one or two empty seats, but all with "occupied" tickets except one.

"How about that one?" I asked, explaining the dilemma of my impending arrest.

"Well, the flight was full, but I'll check," said the officer and walked down the aisle. Time dragged on. I tried out the seat for size. It fitted perfectly! Then I heard what seemed to be the thump of the door closing.

All these long minutes my heart was crying to the Lord and claiming 1 Peter 3:22. The officer reappeared. "I don't understand it, sir. We are supposed to have been full when we left Nairobi, but we have to go. That seat is yours!"

What a sweet sound it is to an old pilot, the surge of the engines on take-off and the "clunk" of the undercarriage that signals we have broken with gravity. But they were never more sweet as I leaned back in my First Class lounging chair to thank God for His timely help. I looked at my watch. It was 2 o'clock. *"Angels and authorities and powers"* and dare I interject—and winds, and airlines— *"being made subject unto Him."*

Soon the aroma of food wafted our way and I didn't realize till then how hungry I was. It had been many hours since we had lifted off from the grass strip at Nyankunde in Zaire. I watched with anticipation as the attendant passed out what appeared to be a delicious steak dinners.

"We seem to be short one meal, sir. Would you mind taking an economy lunch?" the attendant asked apologetically.

"Fine. Thanks." That was better than what I would have been having in Entebbe about now. He passed a steak dinner to a turbaned gentleman across the aisle.

"I don't eat meat," he frowned.

The attendant turned to me with a smile, "Would you oblige, and take this one?" I obliged.

Now there was the ticketing problem. There I was, flying to London on an airline for which I did not have a ticket. I engaged in conversation with the gentlemen beside me and he was most interested in how I ended up in a seat that had been occupied by someone else out of Nairobi. I told him the story as I knew it and of my problem about the tickets. It turned out that he was an airline executive who had been sent to Nairobi to organize the airlift of the fleeing Asians to London.

This was the last such flight and he was going home. He had a bag full of schedules and tickets. "Oh, just leave it to me," he said, "We'll sort it out in London."

Sort it out he did. My tickets were rewritten, connections made, and then, since it was now very late, he arranged a voucher for me to stay the night in the luxurious Gatwick Shelby Hotel.

At last, as I lay back in bed, safe and showered, I could not help but marvel at the gracious intervention of the Lord and of His mighty power. Who was it that stirred up those winds that caused the plane to land and extricate one of His servants from danger? We marvel with the disciples, *"Even the...winds obey Him."* And who was it that occupied that seat from Nairobi to Entebbe and did not return to claim it? How does that verse begin again? *"Angels..."* How did that executive and I get seated together? *"Authorities..."* Why was I not halted at the gate? *"Powers."* All are subject unto Him.

And I did enjoy that steak!

—*J. Boyd Nicholson, March-April 1995, pp. 4-5*

37. The Birds (Gen. 8)

I t is difficult to imagine the scene. For 150 days the world had been engulfed in a raging flood. Every living thing had died, except eight humans and a representative few of every created species. And these were all floating snugly in an ark, on the surface of the flood. From the time God placed those favored beings in the ark and shut the door upon them, they stayed safely enclosed within for a period of about seven-and-a-half months before the waters had receded enough for the tops of the mountains to appear.

In the top of the ark was its only window. We can only conjecture as to whether Noah, from time to time after the rain stopped, opened the window to look about and gauge the progress of the flood. He knew, of course, that all those within the ark were safe and would ultimately be returned to dry ground. He knew also that all those not inside had perished.

Ultimately, as Noah sensed the time approaching for the flood to end, he opened the window one day with a specific purpose. For the first time he would release some of the creatures from the ark. He selected a raven and set it free.

The surface of the water over which the bird flew that day must have been liberally littered with the debris of God's judgment. Logs and trees must have floated in abundance as well as the bodies of thousands of drowned creatures.

We do not know what the raven had been feeding on during its months in the ark. Certainly, nothing had died during the voyage, so its ark diet likely did not include carrion. But, as that raven flew out over the vast littered seascape, its old appetites evidently returned. It forgot all about the ark, even about the mate it had left behind. Though Noah waited, the raven never returned. He knew, of course, that it had to have landed, had to have found food, and evidently was quite satisfied with what it found. Whatever it had found had become more precious to it than the ark it left behind.

Also, perhaps at the same time he sent forth the raven, Noah sent forth a dove. But this bird, whose appetite was very different from that of the raven, found no resting place on the flood waters for the sole of her foot. She fled back to the only place of safety for herself—to Noah and the ark. He was waiting for the dove's return and pulled her back to himself and to safety and camaraderie within.

The world of today is likewise awash in sin and its effects. The debris of wickedness litters the seascape. The savor of death is everywhere. God's judgment is about to fall, engulfing once again the whole creation in His holy wrath.

And today there is a single ark of safety. It floats serenely above the tide of death and decay. All within are safe. But from the haven of safety a window remains open; and from it birds of various feathers fly forth to work, to play, to survey, perhaps even to feed.

We too go forth. We know the security of the ark of safety. Still we fly; driven by the craving or the perceived necessities of life. Well may we ask ourselves—are we like the raven, or like the dove?

Both were sent by Noah. We are sent as well; sent to work, sent to testify, sent to survey the seascape of time. But what do we find in our goings forth? Like the raven, is it the dead things of earth we feed on; the flotsam of a sin-sick world to rest our feet upon? Or are we like the dove, finding no rest, no home, no peace upon those restless waters? Are we, like the dove, happy to return to the ark?

Where our treasure is, there our heart is also. So long as the personal appetite is right, we will always delight to return to the One who is our Noah—the Master of the ark. We will rest where He rests, feed where He feeds. And there we will be safe. But if, like the raven, as we flutter about the seascape of time, our old appetites return, then we shall not do well. We'll forget the ark and the One who sent us forth. We'll feed again on the cold, dead rottenness of earth. We shall drift. And, though our Noah waits for many days, will He have to conclude that we no longer feel at home in the ark?

Where will you feed today? Where is the place of your rest? Is the ark of Christ home and happiness to your weary soul? (see Ps. 37:4).

—*Doug Kazen, March-April 1995, p. 14*

38. Take it Easy!

ounds good, doesn't it? Especially after a rigorous time of physical, emotional, or spiritual expenditure. The disciples surely knew about that when the Master told them to *"Come apart and rest awhile."* The key word there, of course, was *awhile*. This was not retirement—just a brief time of rest and refreshing in the presence of the Lord for their restoration, in view of further labor.

Well-meaning friends look at the busy servant, weary at times, working long hours, *"in journeyings oft,"* and in a kindly way, with a gentle pat on the shoulder, lovingly suggest, "Take it easy, brother! You're not as young as you used to be, you know." Ah! How good it sounds—"easy." But what is "easy"? Is it absence of labor? Is it sitting in the mall, drinking a "cuppa" and watching the people go by? Is it retiring to a quiet spot with no schedule, no pressures, no demands, and a good book—a place in the sun?

The problem with "easy" is that one man's ease can be another man's boredom—laced with a bit of guilt. Busyness relates to capacity. One man's hard labor with perspiration can be another man's wholesome engagement with inspiration. For one, the work can be debilitating; for another, joyously invigorating for himself and for those he serves.

The Lord never promised "easy" to the sinner in his sins. Certainly He offered "simple," but these are not the same. The way of salvation is simple: *"come," "enter," "receive," "call," "believe."* Man in his religiosity compounds the problem and complicates the way—rather, his many ways—to God.

Though simple, God's way is not easy. It is hard for the sinner to acknowledge his sin. It is hard to confess he has been wrong about God all his life. It is hard to believe apart from works, against reason and distinct from emotion. But it is simple:

> *Only a step to Jesus! Believe and thou shalt live;*
> *Lovingly now He's waiting, and ready to forgive.* (F. Crosby)

Actually the Lord never promised "easy" for His servants, either. However, He did promise He would always be there: at hand to help; above to overrule; before to guide; behind to guard; and underneath with His everlasting arms to comfort. The only easy thing He has is His yoke. *"For My yoke is easy, and My burden is light"* (Mt. 11:30). In that context it means, "My yoke fits well."

As the Divine Carpenter, He makes all His yokes *suitable* for each laborer so that they will not be burdened beyond what they are able to bear. As the Divine Comforter, He makes His yokes *smooth* so that they will not irritate. As the Divine Controller, He makes His yokes *strong*, so that they will not break, but stand the rigors of the appointed task.

The word "easy" in Matthew 11:30 is translated *"better"* in Luke 5:39. So His easy yoke is better. It is better than the unequal yoke. It is better than the uneven yoke. It is better than the untried yoke, because it only becomes *"easy"* when we take it upon us.

In Luke 6:35, the word is translated *"kind."* How kind of the Master to provide a yoke that is easy and better than any other. How kind to permit a poor sinner saved by grace to take it up and labor for Him, and with Him. Angels would leave heaven to do this, but they are not commissioned.

In Romans 2:4, the word there is translated *"goodness."* It is one of the "good things" of the Lord. *"...how much more shall your Father which is in heaven give good things to them that ask Him?"* (Mt. 7:11). If we have been asking for a good thing, here is one right at hand, ready to take up—His easy, kind, better yoke.

In 1 Peter 2:3, the word is translated, *"gracious"*—His gracious yoke. We are saved by grace, accepted in grace, and grow in grace. We stand in grace and are gifted by grace. Out of the riches of His amazing grace He offers us the undeserved honor of taking up His easy, better, good, and gracious yoke. Then, in matchless grace He rewards us!

It is a wonderful paradox. *"Take My yoke...find rest."* Not necessarily rest for the body or mind, but *"rest unto your souls."* Soul-rest in the midst of labor. That is what keeps the faithful servants going. They drink deeply of the Fountainhead and refresh others out of the overflow. They ask much of the Father and hilariously give out of the overplus. They take up the yoke and His burden that's light, and overcome. They learn to be like their Master, meek and lowly in heart.

Take it easy? Yes! take it—there it is, right at hand—easy, better, kind, good, and gracious; His very own yoke, made especially for you.

> *Rest is not quitting this busy career,*
> *Rest is the fitting of self to one's sphere.*
> *'Tis loving and serving the Highest and Best;*
> *'Tis onward, unswerving; and this is true rest.*
>
> (J. W. von Goethe)

—J. Boyd Nicholson, Editorial, March-April 1997, p. 3

39. Love's Rendezvous

I t was 9:20 Sunday morning and there came a brisk knock at Mary's door. She opened it and there stood John with a smile on his face. Mary welcomed him into her home and John walked quickly to his favorite chair and sat down. Mary sat down on the couch and waited. She couldn't help noticing how handsome John looked. He was wearing an expensive suit, beautifully tailored; his shoes wore the sheen of careful polishing; his tie and socks were in the best of taste. His hair was neatly combed and he sat erect and tall.

Mary waited. She knew at the proper time John would begin. Promptly at 9:30, John began to speak.

"Mary, you can't realize how much this means to me. All week long I have looked forward to this hour, anticipated it with heart-longing. Now the time has come and I am here, here to tell you how much I love you. Mary, my life is lived for this rendezvous with you each week."

"Ah, Mary, I was thinking back to the day when I first met you. My heart thrilled and I knew you were the one for me. Our courtship days, our wedding—what memories! Sweet memories…"

"I think of the time when I was sick and when you nursed me, losing sleep while you tenderly cared for me. I remember when my fever was raging and when your loving hand cooled my forehead. It was as a breeze from heaven. You nursed me back to health and strength. Without you I would surely have died, Mary."

At this point, John's eyes filled with tears. He stopped, struggling to control his emotions. Pulling out his handkerchief, he dabbed his eyes, then blew his nose vigorously. After a few moments of struggling to restrain his emotion, he regained his composure and continued.

"Mary, as I sit here this Sunday morning, you are more lovely to me than ever before. Your eyes are like limpid mountain pools of clear blue water. Your face is a mirror of loveliness. Your moral character causes me to wonder. I have never known another person who was so loving, kind, thoughtful, just, and upright. Mary, you are wonderful."

"Most of all, Mary, I love you because of what you have done for me. You have stood with me through thick and thin. When I was most in need of you, you sacrificed yourself for me to save my life. Mary, I can never, never thank you enough for what you have done for me. You mean more to me than anything."

"Well, Mary, it is about time for me to go. Looking at my watch, I see that it is nearly 10:30. Oh, how thankful I am for this opportunity to be with you each week. I live for this hour. Now before I go, I want to give you something to express my deep love and gratitude."

At this point, John pulled out his wallet with a flourish. Thumbing past several twenty-dollar bills, he pulled out a crisp new five-dollar bill. Then, with a tender smile, he placed this on the table for Mary.

"Mary, I must be going now. It has been wonderful to be with you, to look into your eyes, and to tell you I love you. Goodbye now until next week. I do love you."

The neighbors watched as John left the house, entered his luxurious new automobile, and drove away. Mary stood in the doorway, watching with tears in her eyes. It was a most unusual marriage. Each Sunday morning this little ritual was repeated.

Gossip spread through the neighborhood. One hour a week did not seem long enough to spend with Mary. John apparently had time for his friends. He was forever going to the beach or mountains. He loved to golf and to bowl. Then, with his clubs and civic affairs, every night seemed filled. Weekends were crowded with trips. In fact, often he was restless at Mary's house, looking forward to the picnic and outing he planned with friends later in the day.

Through the week John never called Mary on the telephone, never wrote her. They almost seemed to live in different worlds, although a good communication system did exist.

Rumor had it that John did not even seem proud of his marriage. When asked if he were married, he would try to change the subject and act embarrassed. In fact, he had even been seen at times with other questionable companions, or so the story went. He seemed to want to appear unattached.

He lived well himself, took special pride in his clothing and car.

After all, in his work one had to make a good impression. A person had to set his sights high to advance in this world. A man has to associate with the big boys if he wants to become one of them. John really lived a little beyond his income trying to keep up with the crowd.

At times he thought of Mary a little and of her needs, but he did give her five dollars each Sunday. True, he had given this amount for the last twenty years and his income had tripled, but then so had his expenses. What a rat race! Well, that's life. And he did love Mary. Each Sunday he put aside one hour for her to tell her of his love. He could spend that time on himself if he so chose. He got up early instead of sleeping in, and fought the traffic to go to see Mary. She should be most grateful. It proved his undying love for her.

The Lord Jesus said long ago, *"This people draweth nigh unto Me with their mouth, and honoreth Me with their lips; but their heart is far from Me"* (Mt. 15:8).

Could this ever be true of any of us?

—*Donald L. Norbie, January-February 1997, pp. 18-19*

40. Jonah and the Worm

here is no doubt that Jonah's life was affected by some great things. The Lord sent him to a great city, with a great message against their great wickedness. Of course we remember Jonah made a great mistake and sought to flee his task. He knew that God was a God of grace and mercy and if the city repented He would spare them—and these were the enemies of Israel. So, Jonah reasoned, if God wants to overthrow the power of Nineveh and punish that pagan people, why not just let Him? So he took off on a cruise and *"paid the fare"*—not realizing just how much this journey was really going to cost him.

To recover His servant and bring him back into His will, the Lord had a few more great things in mind. *"The Lord sent out a great wind."* That mighty storm certainly caught Jonah's attention. God has ways of doing this, since His love for His own is such that He will not sit idly by and watch the disintegration of their lives without doing something.

At last Jonah—and here we see that he did have some compassion—offered himself up as a sacrifice to save the terrified mariners. Those noble sailors did everything they could to avoid offering up Jonah's life as a substitute for them. Finally, all other hope gone, they *"cast him forth into the sea."*

God wasn't finished with great things yet in His work of saving Jonah's life and service. *"The Lord had prepared a great fish to swallow Jonah."* Talk about sheer terror—being swallowed, and slithering down the gullet of that great fish into its warm innards! It was especially prepared by God, no doubt, but it must have been some sort of air-breathing creature or else Jonah would have suffocated.

What a blessing it was for Jonah that he had memorized so much Scripture! His great cry out of the fish was made up of quotations from the Word of God. Little did he realize that, there in that terrifying circumstance, he was being made a sign, not only for the Ninevites, but the only sign the Lord Jesus would give to the unbelievers of His day of His own death and resurrection (Lk. 11:29).

Not too soon, nor yet a moment too late, the Lord gave command to the fish to get rid of Jonah. The Lord's work in him was progressing, though not yet finished. So the fish *"vomited"* Jonah out on dry land. One does not vomit delicately, and what mighty unsavory heavings in the great fish finally ejected poor Jonah on the beach.

At last the Lord's servant gets back into the divine will and goes to Nineveh with the message that they still have forty days to repent. They did, they were spared, and Jonah was angry. Now he presents his petulant prayer to the Lord to take his life away. After all, who would listen to his preaching now? Had the Lord not said about prophets, *"When a prophet speaketh in the name of the Lord, if the thing follow not, nor come to pass, that is the thing which the Lord hath not spoken, but the prophet hath spoken it presumptuously"* (Deut. 18:22)? So what was the point of him living any longer? He had prophesied, and his prophecy of doom was averted by the mercy of God. All his credibility was gone. He had wanted those enemies of God and of Israel to perish. In fact, he still expected them to be destroyed, for he took up a position on the sunrise side of the city to watch its destruction—the death of real people.

Now God will complete His work in His servant. He will teach him the kind of God that He is: He prepared a weed to grow up in a night and, by its large tropical leaves, provided a shelter for Jonah.

The wind, the whale, and the weed were all part of God's plan of recovery. Now *"the Lord prepared a worm."* See that little inchworm wiggling its way through the dust, directed by God, to eat the vitals of the weed so that in a day it died (and the worm didn't even know it did it!). God sovereignty controls the very great and the very least to do His will.

Jonah suffered angrily by the death of the weed. Now he must learn how much more the Lord would suffer if that great city should be destroyed along with its helpless company and guiltless cattle.

If Jonah was afraid of his own reputation, think how often in this present godless world, heading for destruction, the God of heaven is maligned. His suffering love, His great mercy, His tender compassion, His greatest Gift, are each despised and rejected. The Psalmist said it, *"The Lord is good to all: and His tender mercies are over all His works."*

He will use a stormy wind, some mighty creature if need be, or a brief and brittle weed to prove it—even a lowly worm!

> *Great God of wonders! all Thy ways*
> *Display Thine attributes divine;*
> *But the bright glories of Thy grace*
> *Above Thine other wonders shine;*
> *Who is a pardoning God like Thee?*
> *Or who has grace so rich and free?*
>
> (Samuel Davies)

—J. Boyd Nicholson, Editorial, January-February 2000, p. 3

41. Spiritual Hazards

ake heed unto thyself, and unto the doctrine; contin-ue in them; for in doing this thou shalt both save thy-self, and them that hear thee" (1 Tim. 4:16). Paul is not here referring to that aspect of salvation which we call conversion, but rather to the preservation of Timothy and his hearers in the Christian pathway. He knew that the service of God was a hazardous assignment and that many had already been turned aside by the subtleties of the world, the flesh, and the devil. To reinforce his warnings, Paul resorted to a series of exceedingly bold metaphors, some vivid pen-pictures of the spiritual dangers which beset every child of God.

SHIPWRECKED (1:18-20): This is indeed graphic language, and two men are actually mentioned by name. Paul gives the reason for their spiritual shipwreck—they *"thrust from them"* (RV) faith and a good conscience. We might liken them to a mariner throwing overboard his compass and thus landing on the rocks. Several *"good"* things are mentioned in the two epistles to Timothy, and a good conscience must surely be prized above all else.

SNARED (3:7): Taken in its context, this verse refers to the possibility of elders falling into *"the snare of the devil,"* but every Christian is really exposed to the same danger. Satan has snares laid for us each one, and he knows our individual weaknesses. We are all on his "hit list."

Even while engaged in holy pursuits, we may walk into his trap and become an object of ridicule in the eyes of the world. A missionary in Africa was walking along a jungle path and meditating on the Scriptures, when suddenly he walked into a trap set for wild boars. Though unhurt, he was left dangling in the air, a spectacle for all to see!

BURNED (4:1-2): Chapter 3 speaks about the Church being *"the pillar and ground of the truth,"* bearing witness to Christ who is the Truth. But here we learn that *"in the latter times some shall depart from the faith,"* turning their backs on revealed truth and *"giving heed to seducing spirits, and doctrines of devils."* This dealing with the occult, all too common today, is playing with fire, and those who do so are sure to be burned. And where are they damaged? Again it is the conscience that is affected—seared or branded as with a hot iron. This leaves a scar and causes loss of feeling, too.

DISEASED (6:3-5): The word *"wholesome"* (v. 3) has the idea of healthful, while *"doting"* (v. 4) means sick or diseased, being so rendered by some translators. Paul here envisages the type of person who fails to feed his soul on the plain teaching of Scripture, "but is filled with a sickly appetite for disputations and contentions about words" (Williams). With such a disease all kinds of complications set in—envy, strife, railings, etc. It is also highly contagious, so Paul says, *"from such withdraw."*

DROWNED (6:9): The warning here is as much needed today as when Paul wrote. Money is still the cause of all kinds of evil, both private and public. The fault lies not in the money itself but in human greed, which craves for money and must have it at all costs. Think of a man grasping for riches, overstretching himself, and then falling into a foul river where people have drowned in countless numbers and others are still drowning. Even if the man himself is not drowned—no true Christian will ever suffer *"destruction and perdition"*—repeated gulps of the polluted waters may have serious results, especially in the throat. Many a Christian has lost his voice for God through gulping the world's muddied waters.

PIERCED (6:10): The thought of covetousness and its consequences is carried over from the preceding verse, but with a change of metaphor. Here the lure of riches causes people to strike against, or fall on, something sharp which pierces their flesh, with most painful results. We may think of someone carelessly plunging into water and being impaled on a pole driven in by fishermen and covered at high tide. *"Pierced themselves through with many sorrows"* that is, their sorrows were self-inflicted and would never have happened had they put spiritual things first. Hence Paul's plea in the next verse: *"But thou, O man of God, flee these things."*

Christian, walk carefully: danger is near!
On in thy journey with trembling and fear;
Snares from without and temptations within
Seek to entice thee once more to sin.

Christian, walk prayerfully: oft wilt thou fall,
If thou forget on thy Saviour to call;
Safe thou shalt walk through each trial and care
If thou art clad in the armor of prayer.

(Anonymous)

—*W. P. W. McVey, November-December 1994, p. 14*

42. THESE...

 hese shall go away into everlasting punishment" (Mt. 25:46).

THESE...not just these statistics—these things—but these people. Real, living, walking, busy people. These barbers, these taxi-drivers, these telephone operators, these housewives, these business men, these fathers, sons, mothers, daughters.

THESE...who feel pain, remorse, sorrow today. THESE...with eyes in peril of becoming sightless in the gloom of black darkness, to sting with bitter weeping of remorse. THESE...whose hands will forever grasp and clutch and never find.

THESE...with keen minds that will be eternally assailed by the undying worm of memories nothing can erase. THESE...whose hands shall find no work forever, for hope and purpose can no longer be in that awful place.

THESE...have feet that shall stumble forever on the dark mountains that will never be tinted with a sunrise. THESE...to be lost forever and to know it. THESE...who will never be found by angelic search parties in that unfathomable abyss where cries are drowned in the shatterings of eternal storms.

THESE...are the men I talk to about the weather, the government, the price of gas, the wars in Africa, or how to barbecue a steak. These are the women I meet in the PTA, the corporate offices, the laundromat or the supermarket, and chit-chat about soap powder, hair styles, premiums.

THESE...are the kids in my school class I live and joke with, the teachers I meet every day.

THESE...people—nice, decent people—are my mailman, store clerk, hairdresser. THESE...are the common folk with common problems and hopes and fears and plans for the future. THESE...are they who, for some reason, have never trusted in the Lord Jesus Christ for salvation.

But the Bible says THESE...are going away. Away from God. Away from His truth, further and further every day away from the joyous company of the Son of God I profess to love.

THESE...do not cost me one hot tear a day, a sleepless night, nor the price of a package of gospel tracts. THESE...I live with, and laugh with. I loan them my car, my lawnmower, my snow shovel, my notebook or a cup of sugar.

THESE...I presume will still be alive tomorrow. THESE...I am sure "some day soon" will give me the ideal opportunity to tell them about the Saviour. THESE...I will read about one day in the death notices. "So sudden wasn't it, dear fellow, too bad he's away." Yes, too bad...away to hell—forever.

THESE...are the precious souls God has loved and longs to save. Loved so much that He gave up His only begotten, beloved Son to the curse, the crown of thorns, the spittle, the nail, and the cry of abandoned sorrow, *"My God, My God, why hast Thou forsaken Me?"*

THESE...are the souls for whom Jesus gave Himself to die, to open His bosom to the flaming sword of justice that they—we all—deserve. For THESE He went below all the black burning billows of God's wrath against our sin and down and down to the dark drowned depths of the very bottom place.

He has done everything He can do to stop these, so loved, from going AWAY. He cries out, *"Is it nothing to you, all ye that pass by? behold, and see if there be any sorrow like unto My sorrow, which is done unto Me, wherewith the Lord hath afflicted Me in the day of His fierce anger"* (Lam. 1:12). Is it nothing to THEM? Is it nothing to ME?

O God, wake me up,
Melt this heart of ice.
Teach me to weep real tears,
To pray real prayers,
To show real love for THESE my friends,
That by my life and lip,
And love of Christ constraining,
THESE will see and hear
That they can yet be saved,
Before it is too late.
For Thou hast loved them,
Given up Thy Son
To that dread cross, to die
For sinners and for sin,
That THESE might be forever saved,
And never "go away" from Thee,
In time
Or in eternity.

—J. Boyd Nicholson, May-June 2000, p. 18

43. COAL FROM HEAVEN

Perhaps the most remarkable proof, within my personal experience, of the watchful interest shown by our heavenly Father in the details of His children's lives, is furnished by an incident which took place in Iceland early in the days of the First World War.

The German submarine campaign had disorganized shipping between Britain and Iceland. Of the few ships which sailed regularly between the two countries, several had been either mined or sunk by submarines. It became exceedingly difficult for Iceland to obtain sufficient supplies of coal for the winter. The little that was available at Akureyri, in the north of Iceland, was quickly sold at a high price.

A SURPRISE MESSAGE

One of our greatest difficulties was in heating the hall for our meetings. My wife and her maid, who met with difficulties at every turn on account of the absence of coal in the household, made special prayer to God that He would be pleased to supply this pressing need. To me it seemed impossible that this request should be granted. No coal was obtainable in the town, nor was there any prospect of supplies coming at that time of the year from Britain. Still, I believed that the Lord would help us in some way or other over our difficulties. But the Lord did *"exceeding abundantly above all"* that we asked or thought. "With God nothing is impossible."

One evening, early in January, when the heating problem was becoming acute, I received a phone call from Reykjavik. It was the French Consul, who informed me that a French vessel had arrived there and had on board five tons of coal for me. He could give me no information as to the shipper, and wanted to know what to do with the coal, as it had to be disposed of at once. Taken by surprise, I was at a loss what instructions to give, but I promised to contact him next morning.

It was a good thing to have five tons of coal, but it could do us little good in Reykjavik, 200 miles away! There was no prospect of a ship leaving for our port, Akureyri, for some months.

I went to see a coal merchant in the town, and he estimated the cost of shipping the coal from Reykjavik to Akureyri, at current freight charges, to be almost twice the worth of the coal! Then he confided in me that there was a quantity of coal already in the town, but it was the property of a man in Reykjavik, who owned several steam trawlers, and who was jealously hoarding it for his boats the following summer, when coal might be more scarce.

"If you could only get him to take your coal, and let you take five tons of his here!" he said, "but I'm afraid it will be hopeless, for the Akureyri Town Council begged him to sell them coal for the townspeople, and he refused. He won't let anyone touch his coal."

"Who is looking after the coal for him?" I asked. He mentioned a man I knew very well who was the only other coal merchant in the town.

I went straight to his house and put the matter before him. "I want you to phone the owner of this coal and ask him to exchange five tons of coal with me. He could take my coal from the French ship at Reykjavik, and I would take five tons of his here."

"It's not a bit of good!" replied the merchant, "he has refused the urgent request of the Town Council, and he won't even let me have any of it for my use, although I am his friend and agent."

"Well, we'll try, anyway," I said; "if you don't mind phoning, I will pay for the call."

He got a connection with the man in Reykjavik in a surprisingly short time, but on stating my request, met with an abrupt refusal. The man wanted coal in Akureyri, not in Reykjavik.

But while the merchant was telephoning to Reykjavik, I was telephoning to heaven! My friend changed the subject and spoke on the phone about other business for a short time, then reverted to his original request about my coal. The man at the other end asked who it was that wanted to change the coal. After a moment's hesitation, during which I was calling on God to cause him to give way, the man at the other end said, "Oh, very well, let him have it. Tell him to send me a wire tomorrow authorizing me to take over his coal."

I went home that evening the possessor of five tons of coal, probably the only one so fortunate in the whole of the north of Iceland. On arriving home, I found a cable awaiting me from London, informing me of the shipment, and a parcel. The sender's name was unknown to me.

Shortly after this, reports came in that Greenland ice was invading the north coast of Iceland. It often happens that immense fields of ice are carried away by storm or current from the coasts of Greenland and borne towards the south. The action of the waves causes them to break up, and as they proceed further south they gradually melt. Sometimes these icebergs prove dangerous to ships crossing the Atlantic, as in the case of the *Titanic*.

A "MISTAKE" OVERRULED

I had been living thirteen years in Akureyri, and all that time I had never seen an iceberg. This time, however, I was going to see considerably more of them than I cared for. A tremendous frost heralded the approach of the hoary giants, and before long the whole of the north of Iceland where we lived lay in the grip of this icy invader.

Then it was that we traced the wondrous hand of God in leading the consignors of the coal to despatch it to Reykjavik instead of Akureyri. In ordinary circumstances this would have been the wrong thing. However, the One who knew that thousands of square miles of icebergs were on their way to the north of Iceland, and that a stock of coal in Akureyri could be exchanged, caused the senders to despatch the coal to Reykjavik. If they had waited for a ship going direct to Akureyri, the coal could not have reached us until months later, for the ice blockaded us more effectively even than the German submarines.

"SCIENCE" PUT TO THE PROOF

As we needed food as well as fuel, I thought I would sell some of the coal. The local doctor told me that he was very anxious to buy some coal for the hospital. This was not a charitable institution; every service was charged for, so I did not hesitate to sell the coal at the usual price.

145

Although the doctor was not a believer in the Lord Jesus, he was always friendly. I told him how God had sent us the coal. He listened with interest and said when I finished: "Oh! that's easily explained on a scientific basis. It's an interesting instance of telepathy. Your prayers caused thought waves; some sensitive person in Britain received an impression from them, and sent you the coal. It was no answer to prayer as you understand it."

A little later I said, "Let me see, doctor, will you not be in great need of coals for the hospital when these you are now buying are exhausted?"

"Yes, indeed," he replied, "I don't know what I shall do if the weather keeps on like this. I'm doing all I can to get coal, but it is impossible."

"Well," I said, "I will tell you how you can get five tons." He listened with intense interest. I continued: "All you have to do is to think about it as hard as you can and send out some very powerful thought waves. Some sensitive person in Britain or elsewhere will receive an impression from you and send the coals. This, according to you, is the way my coals came, and you ought to be able to do as well. We are now in January. I will give you to the end of March to get your coal."

My friend collapsed. I then informed him in very direct language that he knew as well as I did that all the telepathy in the world would never have brought five tons of coal in such unusual circumstances, and that only the wisdom and power of Almighty God, the Creator of heaven and earth, could possibly have answered our feeble cry and supplied our need. I hope he learned his lesson.

PROOF OF DIVINE GUIDANCE

I heard later that God had so burdened the hearts of some of His children in England with our need of fuel that they, with persistent effort and even personal representations to the Admiralty, were able to obtain permission to send the coal.

The ship decided on was the *Bisp,* a Danish steamer that was to leave for Iceland about that time. For some unknown reason this was changed and the coal was ordered to be sent by the French vessel instead. The *Bisp* ran aground and had to return to dock for inspection and repair. Could human judgment have foreseen this?

Needless to say, this wonderful manifestation of God's care for us greatly strengthened our faith. Every shovelful of coal was a reminder of His faithfulness. Indeed, I may say that it was a blessed lesson to many who knew the circumstances.

—Arthur Gook, November-December 1994, pp. 4-5

44. THE SEED AND THE INFIDEL

There is a photograph of a grave in my files that is most unusual. The grave belongs to a German princess of a bygone day. She was an infidel and when she came to die she raised the final token of her infidelity against God—her last will and testament.

She left on record that her grave was to be covered with a great granite block. This was to be supported around by other blocks and all were to be chained together with heavy iron links. As a last rebellion, there was to be chiseled in the great block the words: "This grave is purchased to eternity and shall never be opened."

However, God does not need a resurrection to open a grave. As the body of this infidel woman was being lowered into its narrow bed, something else went in beside the coffin. From the beech tree that shaded the grave, gracefully and silently floated down a single seed. The body was buried, the grave was closed, and eventually the great stones sealed the body forever in the tomb.

Forever, did I say? Well that was the wish of the ungodly woman who feared to be raised to meet a holy God. No, the grave would not be sealed forever. The little seed that had been buried beside her body possessed something the wealthy princess had no longer, the germ of life.

Soon the seed began its relentless path toward the light, passing without hindrance between the linked stones that weighed heavily upon the earth. Just a green slip it appeared to be, then a stalk, soon a sapling and the irresistible power put into it by the God this infidel woman had rejected began to press the stones apart. Larger grew the tree and the iron links were stretched to the limit. Whether in the black of night or at high noon we cannot tell. It would not surprise us a bit if it took place exactly on the day and the hour of the anniversary of that sad and hopeless funeral, but it happened no doubt with a violent crack. The chains snapped, the stones released, they spread apart, and the tree still grew.

The old photograph I have shows the grave with the tree growing out of it towards that place the tragic infidel will never see. As for the stones, not one of them is in its original position.

The words can still be clearly read in the stone, "This grave is purchased to eternity and shall never be opened." What a solemn testimony to the truth of Galatians 6:7, *"Be not deceived; God is not mocked: for whatsoever a man soweth, that shall he also reap."*

Her grave will be opened yet again, but on that day she will instantly obey the irresistible command to come forth. The Lord has declared it, *"Marvel not at this: for the hour is coming, in the which all that are in the graves shall hear His voice"* (Jn. 5:28). What a coming forth that will be!

The greatest miracle known to man is the raising of the dead. Paul, before Agrippa, asked the people, *"Why should it be thought a thing incredible with you, that God should raise the dead?"* (Acts 26:8). The heart of the issue was that the Jesus whom Paul served had been crucified, but was now seated above, a living Saviour. Paul would witness to them of that great truth from his own experience. He had seen and heard the risen Christ.

The resurrection of Christ is *the basis of our faith: "If Christ be not raised your faith is vain."* Without this foundation, all preaching is empty, our witness is false, believing is groundless, forgiveness is meaningless, and loved ones who have died trusting in Christ have perished (1 Cor. 15:14-19).

That resurrection is *the basis of our hope.* For *"if in this life only we have hope in Christ"* then we have only misery as a companion and there is no hope beyond the grave. *"But now is Christ risen from the dead"* (1 Cor. 15:20). He is our hope.

The resurrection is *the basis of our love,* implicit in three words in 1 Corinthians 15. *"Preaching"* (v. 14) suggests love to the saints, for their edification, exhortation and comfort. *"Witnesses"* (v. 15) suggests love for the lost, in hopes that what has been learned of Christ will persuade men to likewise trust Him. *"Testified"* (v. 15) suggests love for the Lord as we stand for Him and His cause in a hostile world. No wonder we love to sing, *"Hallelujah! Christ arose!"*

Go and search the tomb of Jesus,
Where the Lord of glory lay;
Jesus is not there, but risen
And has borne our sins away.
It is finished! It is finished!
Captive led captivity!

See Him now in heaven seated,
Mark His glory-circled brow;
Death o'er Him hath no dominion,
For He ever liveth now!
Lord, we long for that glad moment,
When to Thee each knee shall bow!
    (R. C. Chapman/A. P. Gibbs)

—J. Boyd Nicholson, Editorial, March-April 2000, p. 3

45. Our Wonderful Bible

o hold a Bible is to grasp a miracle. This Book is miraculous in its *preparation*—penned by more than 40 writers over a period of approximately fifteen hundred years. It is miraculous in its *presentation*, integrating the works of this diversity of writers into a consistent unit without error or contradiction in the original documents, the autographs. It is miraculous in its *preservation* as accurately copied, handwritten manuscripts. It is miraculous in its *proclamation*—a message from God, empowered and inspired by His Spirit.

The word "Bible" comes from the Greek *biblos*, meaning "a book." The divinely directed continuity of "The Book" unites the sixty-six individual books into what we know as the Old and New Testaments. Both the sacred writings of the Old Testament (Mt. 21:42; Jn. 5:39; Rom. 11:2; 2 Tim. 3:15, etc.) and of the New Testament (2 Pet. 3:15-16) are declared to be *"the Scriptures,"* therefore, according to 2 Timothy 3:16, inspired by God.

It was not until AD 400, approximately 300 years after John lifted his pen at the conclusion of the Book of Revelation, that Jerome compiled the entire Bible into a Latin version known as the Vulgate. In this generally unknown language, the Word of God was hidden from the common people for almost another thousand years. Aldhelm, first bishop of Sherborne in Dorset, is said to have translated the Book of Psalms into Old English soon after 700 AD. However, it was not until about 1380 AD that John Wycliffe, using the Vulgate text, completed a translation of the New Testament into English. His friends completed his unfinished work on the Old Testament after his death in 1384.

Before the invention of the printing press in 1425, all copies of the Scriptures were laboriously reproduced by hand. The first major work from Gutenberg's press was the Latin Bible in 1456, but William Tyndale's translation of the New Testament, issued in 1525, was the first English New Testament to be set in type. He published his version of the Pentateuch in 1530, but his work on the remainder of the Old Testament was terminated by his martyrdom.

We are especially privileged in the twentieth century. The development of printing technology and the diligent work of many scholars has resulted in a profusion of study helps and translations of the Scriptures in the English language, particularly. This rich legacy, of course, proportionally increases our responsibility to use it for the spiritual benefit of ourselves and others.

Unfortunately not all the books and other materials at our disposal provide wholesome teaching. Therefore, the Scriptures themselves must be the ultimate standard of truth. Caution is also essential in our use of the versions of the Scriptures now available. Distinguish between paraphrases of the Scriptures and versions that accurately translate the wording of the original text. While paraphrases are useful, they are, strictly speaking, interpretations, rather than translations. Since we believe the actual words of the original to have been divinely inspired, accurate literal translations which follow that wording convey the meaning of the original text are to be preferred for study. Advice from mature believers is valuable when selecting a Bible for study.

The danger is that we who enjoy such easy access to the Bible may fail to appreciate its worth. The generally frantic pace of life in the so-called "developed" nations often make it difficult to set aside time to read the Word of God, much less to seriously study and meditate on it. When we do invest hours to this commitment, we begin to realize how extensive and rewarding the study of this Book can be—yet how miniscule is our largest grasp of its grandeur after all.

The Lord in His wisdom has provided godly teachers for His people (Eph. 4:7-16). We should take advantage of every opportunity to listen to them, read their writings, and use this material for our spiritual growth. To maximize our benefit from the Word of God, however, we must allow the Holy Spirit to confirm what we learn from others by directing our personal study of the Bible and by helping us to capture its truths for ourselves.

Scripture is our source of spiritual nourishment; prayer and fellowship with other Christians enhance its effectiveness. Peter calls it milk (1 Pet. 2:2) to be eagerly desired. However, only spiritual infants rely entirely on milk (Heb. 5:13) and Paul encourages us to mature, extending our spiritual diet to include the *"meat"* (1 Cor. 3:2; cf. Heb. 5:14). As we know, food must be both eaten and digested to be of nutritional value. We derive benefit from the spiritual nourishment available in the Bible only when we read it retentively, study it seriously, and apply it appropriately.

Space will allow only a short review of the doctrine of inspiration and the history of the preservation of the Scriptures. Wider reading in the many books written on the subject would be interesting and helpful. Assurance of the authority and ageless applicability of these God-given documents is an encouragement for us to diligently explore the truths they contain.

—Gary Seale, September-October 1994, p. 8

46. The "Me First" Syndrome

 uffer me first..." This was the language of one of the Lord's disciples. Not an enemy, not a disinterested listener, but *"another of His disciples."*

In response to the verbal commitment of one of the scribes, the Lord Jesus, the Lord of life and glory, Sovereign of the skies, said, *"The foxes have holes, and the birds of the air have nests; but the Son of man hath not where to lay His head."* It is shocking that this One, who is God's *"dear Son,"* the Creator of all things *"that are in heaven, and that are in earth,"* had not a place to lay down His head!

He had just healed a leper with a touch, the centurion's servant with a word, and Peter's wife's mother by reaching out His hand. Shortly He would rebuke the wind and calm the stormy sea. Surely this One of such power and authority could make for Himself a comfortable little place where He could *"lay His head."* One word of command and there it would be, comfortably located in Capernaum by the seaside. But such thoughts of serving Himself first—or even last—were never considered in the mind of the Lord Jesus.

One standing by heard those words that conveyed the homelessness and loneliness of the Master, and without waiting to hear any more, interjected, *"Suffer me first."* The Lord had not yet addressed him, but it seems the disciple knew what was coming. It would be a call to *put the Lord first* and follow Him. That was not quite what was in the disciple's mind. He had the *"me first"* syndrome.

It is the curse of the day in the ungodly world around us. Self-will, self-promotion, and self-attention are praised as positive attributes to "get ahead." That is, to get ahead of *others.* "Me first" is the clarion call of carnality while others are trampled, jostled, pushed aside, and hurt in the process.

"But surely," one objects, "I can have my own mind." Well, No! Not if you are a disciple. *"Let this mind be in you, which was also in Christ Jesus."* Until we lay our mind and its persistent self-will at the feet of the Master in holy exchange for His mind and will, we will never know peace nor gain a victory in the war that goes on continually within us. The battle is between *"the law of sin which is in [our] members"* and *"the law of [the] mind."*

Whether we yield to "me" or to the Master determines which standard will fly at the ramparts of our lives: *"...Me first"* or *"Jesus Christ our Lord."*

The mighty apostle knew the battle well (Rom. 7). But the blessed Lord Jesus never knew this battle. There was nothing in Him that could respond to selfishness. He is the First, but He put Himself last. He is the Greatest, but He made Himself least. He is the Highest, but He washed His disciples' feet.

He made all things, *"that are in heaven, and that are in earth, visible and invisible, whether they be thrones, or dominions, or principalities, or powers,"* but when it came to making something for Himself, He *"made Himself...no reputation."* He who possesses all things, when it came to taking something for Himself, He *"took...the form of a servant."*

"A servant." Ah, that's the problem—the servant spirit. We all love to *be* served, and there is no doubt about it, it is nice. But do we love as earnestly to *be* the servant? My son used to make a statement, "You'll know you're a servant when they treat you like one," but recently he put his finger on the real problem we all face: "You'll know you're a servant by *the way you react* when they treat you like a servant." The battle is not what we do in our service, but how we think. It is the battle of the mind—peace or perplexity, turmoil or tranquility.

In Exodus 21 there are two servants. One served in love for his master and would not go out free. He became a marked man *"for ever."* The other fully discharged his obligation, did his duty, and then went out free *"for nothing."*

How deeply this convicts the writer. Will it be devotion or duty, liberty or love, *"for ever"* or *"for nothing,"* "Thee first" or "me first"?

What drives me onward to serve, day by day?
Is it something for me, or glory for Thee?
What motive enlivens each nerve in the fray?
Is it THEE, my God, is it THEE?

What is it draws my first love to impart?
Is it something for me, or THEE, only THEE?
What is it below or above fills my heart?
Is it THEE, my God, is it THEE?

Help me to more understand by Thy grace,
That the best thing for me, is enjoyment of THEE;
That blessings and service, though grand in their place,
Are not THEE, blessed God, are not THEE.

—J. Boyd Nicholson, Editorial, September-October 1999, p. 3

47. THE WORTHY WALK

hen the patriarch Abram was ninety-nine years old, *"the Lord appeared to Abram, and said unto him, I am the Almighty God; walk before Me, and be thou perfect"* (Gen. 17:1).

"That ye might walk worthy of the Lord unto all pleasing, being fruitful in every good work, and increasing in the knowledge of God" (Col. 1:10).

You can tell a good deal about a person by the way he walks. Everyone's walk is distinctive. No one walks exactly the way you do. You reveal a good deal about your character by the way you walk, by where you walk, with whom you walk, and in many other ways.

In the Bible, the walk is used to figure the character of a man's life, and God has some wonderful promises which are dependent on the way we walk. For example, *"No good thing will He withhold from them that walk uprightly"* (Ps. 84:11).

Walking has to do with the day-by-day living that characterizes our lives. It is not in the rush-and-go, the excitement of the chase and the race, that our lives are best viewed. *"The race is not to the swift, nor the battle to the strong"* (Eccl. 9:11).

It is in the day-by-day plodding, one step at a time, on the journey of our life that our characters are best viewed. We are required to take only one step at a time and not to cross bridges until we come to them.

In one of the earliest mentions of walking, we read twice in Genesis 5:22 and 5:24 that Enoch walked with God. Enoch's name means "tuition," and the man that walks with God is taught of God.

The two on the road to Emmaus didn't know that it was Jesus Himself who *"drew near and went with them."* But they did know afterwards that He had taught them many wonderful things from the Word of God as He opened both the Scriptures and the eyes of their understanding.

We read that Enoch walked with God after he begat Methuselah. A new life ought to be characterized by a change in the walk. Enoch walked with God for 300 years after his son was born. He didn't choose the direction of his life—he walked with God. God chose the path, the purpose, and the prospect of his walk.

> *We cannot always trace the way*
> *Where Thou, our gracious God dost move;*
> *But we can always surely say*
> *That God is love.*

After his 300 years of walking with God and witnessing for God (Jude 14-15), Enoch was taken Home by the Lord. He *"was translated that he should not see death"* and *"before his translation he had this testimony, that he pleased God"* (Heb. 11:5).

How can we please God? By the way we walk. Enoch furnishes us the clue, because we read twice over, *"he walked with God."*

In the Epistle of the Ephesians, we read a great deal about walking. In Ephesians 4:1, we are exhorted to walk worthy of the calling wherewith we are called. The Christian's walk should be different, and his talk should be different. We should evidence that we are the Lord's, both by what we do and what we say.

We read that we are saved by grace through faith, not of works lest any man should boast, *"for we are His workmanship, created in Christ Jesus unto good works, which God hath before ordained that we should walk in them"* (Eph. 2:10).

Also it is written, *"Be not drunk with wine, wherein is excess; but be filled with the Spirit; speaking to yourselves in psalms and hymns and spiritual songs, singing and making melody in your heart to the Lord"* (Eph. 5:18-19). When a man is drunk, both his walk and his talk are affected; and when a man is filled with the Spirit, he'll have something to say and do to help his brother in Christ; he will be singing and praising God in both heart and life.

Ephesians 5 tells us that there are three ways that the believer should walk: *"Walk in love, as Christ also hath loved us, and hath given Himself for us..."* Christ not only declared His love for His own, but He demonstrated it.

Even with the cross immediately before Him, He took a humble servant's place and washed His disciples' feet, He told them, *"I have given you an example that you should do as I have done to you"* (Jn. 13:15). *"Christ also suffered for us, leaving us an example, that ye should follow His steps"* (1 Pet. 2:21). No better example could be given by Him who said, *"Love one another as I have loved you."*

In Ephesians 5:8, we read, *"Ye were sometimes darkness, but now are ye light in the Lord; walk as children of light."* The Lord reminded His disciples, *"As long as I am in the world, I am the Light of the world:"* but, in His absence, *"Ye are the light of the world."* The only light the world has comes through the Scriptures and through His people, so we are exhorted to *"shine as lights in the world, in the midst of a crooked and perverse generation."* The Lord further tells us: *"Men loved darkness rather than light, because their deeds were evil"* (Jn. 3:19), but *"He that doeth truth cometh to the light, that his deeds may be made manifest, that they are wrought in God"* (v. 21).

"If we say that we have fellowship with Him, and walk in darkness, we lie, and do not the truth: but if we walk in the light, as He is in the light, we have fellowship one with another, and the blood of Jesus Christ His Son cleanseth us from all sin" (1 Jn. 1:6-7).

"See then that ye walk circumspectly, not as fools, but as wise, redeeming the time, because the days are evil" (Eph. 5:15). This means to be looking around, aware of the dangers on every hand. The watchword of the Christian is "Watch your step!"

We are to *"abstain from the very appearance of evil."* The things which do not appear right are to be as scrupulously avoided as those things which are clearly wrong. We should not ask, "What's wrong with it?" but "What's right with it?" The Lord leads in the *"paths of righteousness for His Name's sake."*

The Bible says, *"He that walks with wise men shall be wise."* Let us, then, walk in fellowship with the Lord and with those of like precious faith, made wise unto salvation through faith in Christ Jesus.

Psalm 1 assures us: Oh, the happinesses of *"the man that walketh not in the counsel of the ungodly...his delight is in the law of the Lord; and in His law doeth he meditate day and night."*

When we walk aright, we live aright. The right prayer for all of us to pray is: *"Search me, O God, and know my heart: try me, and know my thoughts: and see if there be any wicked way in me, and lead me in the way everlasting"* (Ps. 139:23-24).

—*Elliot Van Ryn, July-August 1994, pp. 16-17*

48. Autumn Glory

ushels of corn, bundles of gladiola, bunches of grapes, and burning leaves all seem to send out a signal to me each year about this time that the summer is ended and the harvest is past. This is not a sad thing for me because there is always something especially beautiful about the autumn in our part of the country.

Crimson and gold leaves emblazoned against blue skies delight the viewer and inspire the artist. The only negative thing is that it is so brief. Only a few weeks, then comes the rain and winds that tear the leaves from the trees, leaving only stark skeletons to face the winter snows.

Old age is really the autumn of life and should, for the believer in Christ, be radiant and rich in the joy of life and full of the fruit of long fellowship with God. *"...It shall come to pass, that at evening time it shall be light"* (Zech. 14:7).

I knew a man like that. He lived for 96 years. A working man until into his 70's, he shepherded the flock of God for over 60 years in the place where he spent most of his life. He rejoiced among the saints and was a benediction to his family.

Since *"Better is the end of a thing than the beginning thereof,"* it is clearly important to finish well. Not all do. Some fall by the way and others end in the gall of bitterness and full of a self pity that makes their company and conversation a burden even to those who love them. What, then, is the secret of a happy life and a radiant old age that blesses the saints like a golden sunset?

That was the question I put to the old veteran. His reply was as uncomplicated as his life. "Satisfaction," he replied, "first with the Lord Jesus Christ. If we are truly satisfied with Him, we will be satisfied with His provision." I knew this man for over forty years and can testify that this was no trite piece of religious jargon, but the expression of a life lived according to that principle and manifested in qualities which, it seems to me, should characterize all who belong to the Lord. Some of these were:

• A THANKFUL SPIRIT: "Lots to be thankful for" was a daily expression for him even when times were tough. Thanklessness breeds discontent and leads to departure from God, as the heathen in Romans 1 discovered to their grief.

• A GOSPEL ZEAL: He never lost his freshness in the gospel, so that very few ever escaped his company without hearing a word of joyful testimony.

When we took him at the last into the emergency ward of the hospital, while the nurse was plugging him into the life-support system, he was plugging the gospel into her! He had learned what many forget today, and some deny, that while *"the preaching of the cross is to them that perish, foolishness...unto us **which are saved** it is the power of God."*

• A LOVE FOR THE WORD OF GOD: This old believer learned at an early age that there is no substitute for the daily reading of the Word. In old age, when studying is past, there is a rich resource of Bible knowledge on which to draw at all times.

• A LOVE FOR THE PEOPLE OF GOD: Some think that when they retire then they will get around to visiting and helping the Lord's people and winning a few souls. Well, it is most unlikely that suddenly we will have a care for the flock of God in old age if we have not felt their burdens throughout our lives. Many older ones keep young in heart by caring for others; even their mental alacrity and physical well-being can know the benefit of this ministry.

• AN APPRECIATION OF THE LORD'S SUPPER: The worshipful spirit will always be full and have some spiritual sustenance to impart. That is a divine principle. When God gets His portion first, then He will respond lavishly with spiritual blessings in heavenly places in Christ.

These qualities, bound together by faith and prayer provided for that old soldier of the Cross a happy, fruitful, and contented life. He lived to see the salvation of each of his children, all his grandchildren, and his great-grandchildren as they came one by one to the years of understanding.

Was he rich? He surely was. Not in the gold of man's mining but in the true riches that withstand the impact of death and the collapse of the universe.

Since these principles worked so well for him and countless others, should we not follow his example? If we do, we can expect to enjoy what he found: *"At evening time it shall be light."*

> *Eye hath not seen, tongue hath not told,*
> *And ear hath not heard it sung,*
> *How buoyant and bold,*
> *Though it seems to grow old,*
> *Is the heart, forever young;*
> *Forever young—though life's old age*
> *Hath every nerve unstrung:*
> *The heart, the heart is a heritage*
> *That keeps the old man young!*
>
> (Author Unknown)

—*J. Boyd Nicholson, Editorial, September-October 1997, p. 3*

49. A Name Problem?

ore and more people have a personal name problem. For some, it is that their name is showing up in places where they would rather be unknown—such as the Internet, indicating that their privacy is perhaps being invaded. Meanwhile, others fret that they are unknowns on earth and they think nobody cares.

The little speck of stellar dust on which we live is one of nine relatively small planets circulating around a medium-sized star in the Orion arm of a spiral galaxy called the Milky Way. Our sun is but one of an estimated 200 billion bright stars. That is, more stars than all the people who have ever lived. These stars together make up, not the heavens, but just our galaxy.

If we try to visualize this vast galaxy in yet another way, consider this: if the stars of the Milky Way were each reduced to the size of a grain of rice, there would be enough such grains to fill all the space in Seattle's King Dome, a covered stadium seating more than 60,000 people!

All this is only our celestial neighborhood. Astronomers believe that the Milky Way is just one of hundreds of billions of such galaxies and that each galaxy is composed of between 100 million and 3 trillion stars. And yet, every one of those countless stars is known to, and has been named by, your heavenly Father. We read in Psalm 147:4-5: *"He telleth the number of the stars; He calleth them all by their names. Great is our Lord, and of great power, His understanding is infinite."*

Well, those are stars—but what about me? Does this great, eternal God of the universe have any thought towards a nondescript human, mingling among the masses of earth, as gravity holds him on this spinning speck in the midst of a smallish solar system that is part of a medium size galaxy that exists as a part of the unnumbered billions of the stars that God Himself has named?

Isaiah knew the answer. In Isaiah 43:1, God declares, *"I have called thee by thy name."* A personal link has been forged between this eternal God who knows the name of every star and the most insignificant of His children. To that child, He extends the certification of His call: *"I have called* **thee**...."

Then He takes His act of personal identification a step beyond what He tells us of the stars. He adds, *"Thou art Mine."* Yes, He made the stars and He named the stars, but it seems that the stars that He made will one day be swept away by His mighty power, when the heavens themselves shall *"pass away with a great noise"* (2 Pet. 3:10). But not one child of His will ever cease to be His loved and personal possession. He declares, *"I have even called thee by thy name. I have surnamed thee, though thou hast not known Me"* (Isa. 45:4). You may respond by saying that this promise is to Israel. But in the context it is to Cyrus, a pagan king! If God's bond of identity extends to him—a king selected to do God's will on earth—how much more does that bond extend to His Bride, who, in the wondrous privilege of her relationship, is *"the fullness of Him that filleth all in all"* (Eph. 1:23)!

Might He not forget me? Is it not likely that He will take more note of great preachers, great theologians, great soul winners, famous missionaries, the great saints and the holy, than of me? Can my name somehow be removed from His favor?

In the vast cataclysm of judgment, when the door of grace closes and the thunder of a holy God breaks the seals, when the trumpets sound and death engulfs the millions who have rejected and forgotten God, might He then just possibly forget me? No! I cannot be forgotten, for the name of every child of God is written indelibly and eternally in the Lamb's Book of Life that lies open to divine scrutiny in heaven. There is written the name of every one whom He has identified by His grace, as His own. Once we are *"in Christ"* no eraser can ever touch that name! It glows upon the eternal record with a greater brilliance, a richer value, a more eternal endurance than the name of any star the God of heaven has ever christened.

There is more, for even now, while your heart aches, while you may be ignored even by those you love, your name is written on the palm of the Hand that made the stars (Isa. 49:16), the Hand that all the combined power of humankind can neither stay nor turn. The Hand that made the stars, the Hand that rules the universe, is engraved with the name of every child that belongs to Him!

Indeed, were we to survey the value that He places on our personal identity, were we to absorb the truth of our eternal association with Him, we would then fulfill the charge given by our Lord in Luke 10:20, *"But rather rejoice, because your names are written in heaven."* Yes indeed! Above the stars, beyond the stars, more personal to Him than any star is the name of every child of God that has been bought by the blood of His Son.

—Doug Kazen, November-December 1996, pp. 12-13

50. A Song in the Wilderness

 ome of the sweetest songs have been wrung out of life's bitterest trials. Many a song that is sung in the sunlight was composed in the darkest of the night watches. Such is Psalm 61.

David's beloved yet rebel son had betrayed him. His trusted counselor conspired against him. His beloved people rejected him, and he fled for his life into the wilderness.

In his lonely distress he sends up a shrill cry into the heavens. But it appears his cry is plagued with doubts: *"Hear my cry."* Many would be crying to the God of heaven from different places at that moment, but was God hearing his personal cry? If He did hear, was He paying any attention to it? *"Attend unto my prayer."*

He seemed to be at such a far distance from God and from God's house. *"From the end of the earth will I cry unto Thee."* Not *"the ends of the earth"* for if at one of the ends, there would always be another end. David feels he is at the very end, the extremity. At *"the end,"* it seems there is no other place to go but out.

How many times a child of God has felt as David, and the enemy would hasten those thoughts of doubt and despair. Among the multitude of cries ascending to heaven, does God actually hear my cry, and if He does, is He paying any attention to it?

Of course, in New Testament times we have the assurance of such scriptures as 1 John 5:14-15, *"And this is the confidence that we have in Him, that, if we ask anything according to His will, He heareth us: and if we know that He hear us, whatsoever we ask, we know that we have the petitions that we desired of Him."*

While David may have felt far from Jerusalem and the place of worship, the child of God has the abiding promise of the Lord, *"He hath said, I will never leave thee, nor forsake thee."* Whether we feel His presence or not, His promise is unfailing and in this we must simply trust.

Not only did David feel at a distance from God, he also felt a sense of despair in his circumstance. *"My heart is overwhelmed,"* he cries.

The word *"overwhelmed"* is *"wrapped in gloom."* What were the matters that had brought him to such a condition?

Perhaps it was physical distress. *"And David went up by the ascent of mount Olivet, and wept as he went up, and had his head covered, and he went barefoot: and all the people that was with him covered every man his head, and they went up, weeping as they went up"* (2 Sam. 15:30). That weeping, barefoot man climbing the slope of Olivet didn't look much like a king that day!

Perhaps adding to his distress was his disappointment in trusted friends. Ahithophel had been his counselor—the man to whom David had opened his heart. Now the word had come, *"Ahithophel is among the conspirators"* (2 Sam. 15:31). What a painful sorrow when a close friend, one who is privy to the innermost feelings of the heart, turns against you. In another psalm, David laments, *"Yea, mine own familiar friend, in whom I trusted, which did eat of my bread, hath lifted up his heel against me"* (Ps. 41:9). How many tears have flowed down the faces of the Lord's people over broken friendships, of ill reports and slanderous criticism.

On top of this, disappointment in his own family added to David's distress. *"And David said to Abishai, and to all his servants, Behold, my son, which came forth of my bowels, seeketh my life"* (2 Sam. 16:11). There are few sorrows to equal that of fathers and mothers brokenhearted over wayward children.

Perhaps weary in the wilderness and feeling vulnerable to attack, David had sat down for rest and shade under a tree, and lifted his eyes to see a great high crag, a veritable natural fortress. He was a soldier and he knew the value of a high vantage point. Suddenly he realized he had a Rock of refuge wherein he would be safe, the Lord God Himself. Too high for him to reach by his own efforts, he longed for the Lord to lead him there. This is the place of refuge, relief, refreshing and restoration.

When he got to that Rock, he would find out what Hannah discovered, *"Neither is there any rock like our God."* He is the Great Incomparable. He would discover what Balaam found when his eyes were opened and he saw the children of Israel from the high rock at Peor, that God's people were beautiful. If I have a critical spirit toward the Lord's people, I need to get some altitude in my life, and see them from God's point of view, discovering that, in spite of their flaws and failings, they are by grace, *"the riches of the glory of His inheritance"* (Eph. 1:18).

At the Rock, David would discover what Moses sang about, that there he could *"suck honey out of the Rock"* (Deut. 32:13). May our heartcry be: *"Lead me to the Rock that is higher than I."*

> *Majestic sweetness sits enthroned*
> *Upon the Saviour's brow;*
> *His head with radiant glories crowned,*
> *His lips with grace o'erflow.*

> *No mortal can with Him compare*
> *Among the sons of men;*
> *Fairer is He than all the fair*
> *That fill, the heavenly train.* (Samuel Stennett)

—*J. Boyd Nicholson, Editorial, May-June 1998, p. 3*

51. The Coats He Wore

f there is a *holiest of all* in the Old Testament writings, it is the golden passional of Israel in Isaiah 52:12–53:12, the song of the suffering Messiah. In the New Testament the high priestly prayer of the Lord Jesus in John 17 compares, a glimpse into the heart of the Son of God conversing with the Father. And Philippians 2, this often considered passage on the downward and upward steps of humiliation and exaltation, is another such place. Our shoes are off to consider it.

One of Paul's major themes in Philippians is conduct becoming the gospel, and that gospel focused on our lives means the very mind of Christ in us. It was not just as a cure for their lack of unity and accord that Paul presents the Lord Jesus in this lovely way. It is so that gospel truth might be worked out in all experiences, under all circumstances. The key to Christ living His life in us begins with the mind that He had to do the Father's will.

The progress in the life of Joseph, as shown by the various coats he wore, illuminates this passage for us. Joseph's coat of many colors was taken from him and exchanged for a servant's garment in Egypt. This was put off when he was sent to wear the covering of a slave in prison. Then later, brought out of prison, he changed his raiment and appeared as the seer to interpret the Pharaoh's dream. Then he was exalted to wear the linen vestures of a sovereign at the Pharaoh's right hand. These coats he wore picture for us the Lord Jesus in His pathway from glory to humility and back to glory.

At the end of Joseph's story, after all his experiences—from being sold into Egypt by his brethren to exaltation at the Pharaoh's right hand—Joseph said to his brethren: *"But as for you, ye thought evil against me; but God meant it unto good, to bring to pass, as it is this day, to save much people alive."* We don't know when this truth dawned upon Joseph's soul. It was an enormous faith to believe what Paul would later call all believers to know—that God does work all things together for good to those who love Him and are called according to His purpose (Rom. 8:28). Perhaps Joseph knew it as early as his dreams of having all the family bow before him. But his behavior throughout his life shows us a man who lives in the conscious knowledge of this. The eye of God is on him for good. He takes that and endures whatever he must.

Living in the consciousness that the eye of God is upon you is the mark of a spiritual believer. This is the man God can use to save many alive, to bring repentance to a nation, to bring glory to God.

THE COAT OF THE SON

The many-colored coat of Joseph was undoubtedly beautiful. It would be a long-sleeved robe that reached to the ankles and marked him out among his brethren as having the birthright which Reuben had forfeited (1 Chron. 5:1-2). We recall that were it not for the deceit of Laban, Joseph would have literally been the firstborn. His brothers hated him for the place of honor given to him. They hated him even more for the revelation that confirmed he would have the first place, when he dreamed of their sheaves bowing to his sheaf. The dreams and the coat given him, however, only verified what Joseph was within. He had it in his heart to follow God's will without resistance. But Joseph was taken by his brethren and sold into Egypt as a slave. They left him to die in a pit with no water, and when they saw the anguish of his soul, they ignored him.

Now we may see the progress of the Son of God in the same five coats that Joseph wore. This coat of colors had a glory that marked out Joseph as the firstborn, with all the accompanying honors. Its outward display matched all that the man was within, as looking to the good that God would do.

This points to the Son of God being in the form of God. That form had nothing to do with shape or external appearance, but with essence. It is an expression of being that carries with it the exact character within. Something like a tennis player who we say is in great form. Implied in that saying is more than the appearance of his backhand. The trained mind and disciplined moves make up that form. This comes from his essence as a devoted professional.

The Son of God was and ever is God in essence: "An external form truly indicative of the inner nature from which it springs." That

171

never changes. But part of the expression of that deity was the homage and glory due to Him, in the spiritual realm of heaven from the angelic hosts. This was the part of His being in the form of God that He deemed a thing not to be grasped at. He would relinquish this visible glory willingly because the Father desired Him to. The only thing that Joseph said during this awful trial in his life of being sold into Egypt, is his response to the father who sent him to Dothan for his brethren, *"Here am I."* Like the coat of colors laid aside, the outward testimony of what Christ always continued to be—glorious deity, essence of God—was now veiled from mortal view.

THE COAT OF A SERVANT

Now Joseph had his coat of colors brutally wrenched from him when he was cast into a pit and sold into Egypt, where he eventually put on the coat of a slave. The firstborn of Jacob's household became a servant in the house of Potiphar. But the Saviour willingly laid aside the coat of heaven's glory. So where is the parallel? In this: when the Son of God did so, He took another form to Himself, the form of a servant. Again it is not an outward shape but an attitude within which will manifest itself.

We should realize that in Philippians 2:7, *"took upon Him the form of a servant"* is *"having taken the form of a servant."* The grammatical construction is such that this action goes ahead of *"made Himself of no reputation."*

So the second point in this change that the Son of God effected is that He took the form of a servant. In His essence, He took to Himself this heart and mind of a servant unto God, even before His incarnation. Because a servant was what was needed to redeem man, a servant of both God and man—for us—He would now express from within a servant character.

The angels beheld that attitude before He became a man. Little wonder that those hosts praised His arrival to the shepherds of Judea when He became a man. That is where the experience of Joseph in the pit and being sold into Egypt comes in. It depicts the foreknowledge of the Son of God concerning all that servanthood would mean to Him.

His Israelite brethren would sell Him, and it rightly illustrates His thoughts as He takes to Himself the form of a servant. Remember that through this whole passage of scripture, an exhortation flows from the mind of Christ, *"Let this mind be in you..."* (v. 5).

What a lesson for our lives is here. Of ourselves, we have only the vainglory of life to cling to. Paul's esteem as an apostle was not something that kept him from the defense and confirmation of the gospel. That landed him in prison, languishing in bonds; some even preached Christ in such a way as to further demean his position and add affliction (1:15-16). Yet he gloried that Christ was preached.

Those coats the Saviour wore touched Paul's life and his mission for God.

THE COAT OF A SLAVE

When Potiphar's wife wickedly tempted Joseph to lie with her, the man who knew the eye of God upon him answered, *"How can I do this great wickedness and sin against God?"* This shows the mind of Joseph as to his service. He fled, leaving behind his coat.

Falsely accused of sin, Joseph was put into prison with the king's prisoners. He never would have thought he would shed his servant's coat like this and become a common prisoner. But the Lord was with him even there, and he wore the prisoner's coat with a view to glorifying God. He was still a servant in spirit, though a prisoner.

The Saviour became the willing bondslave when He donned the coat of humanity. *"He was made in the likeness of men."* In this act, He emptied Himself. In His incarnation He divested Himself of the garment of visible glory that was His as verily God.

Being in the attitude of a servant, and in the likeness of men, it was not possible to receive on earth the spiritual appreciation of His essential deity that He did in heaven. His essential deity was unchanged and just as real, but only faint glimpses of that glory were seen. John said they beheld it, *"the glory as of the only begotten of the Father, full of grace and truth"* (Jn. 1:14). But grace and truth were for men, and as marvelously as Jesus displayed them, this was only part of the form of God which was rightly His.

This done, He humbled Himself in obedience to the death of the cross. This is our essential gospel—not only for men to come and be saved, but to go on to perfection. This is gospel living. So Christ was like Joseph in that He was accused falsely, but unlike him, in that as a prisoner He died.

Notice that He was obedient to the death of the cross, not unto death. This means that His obedience included laying down His life willingly that He might take it again. Death had neither claim nor hold on Him. When the Lord Jesus died, death at last found a victim that it didn't know what to do with, for it had not the claim upon Him that it had on all others who had passed that way.

Joseph was a prisoner all the while the king had an entirely wrong impression about him and what he was. In this sense we may say the Lord Jesus wore the prisoner's coat all the days of His earthly sojourn. For from His appearance at Jerusalem when He was twelve until He gave up the spirit on the cross, the world and the princes of this world knew Him not. They never knew that the wisdom of God was unfolding before them. Had they known it, they would not have crucified the Lord of glory. In that sense He was always a falsely accused man. And the world at large continues to have a false impression of His glorious person and work.

Appropriately enough, Paul, when writing this passage (1 Cor. 2:8), was a prisoner, condemned for no good cause and completely misunderstood in his identification with the Christ of these coats. But he was ready to say that his afflictions were all needed for the furtherance of the gospel, for he knew the coats he wore.

THE COAT OF THE SEER

When the chief of butlers and the chief of bakers were imprisoned with Joseph, they told Joseph of a dream they had. Joseph's mind was still set on God, for his answer to their sadness at not knowing the interpretation of the dream was, *"Do not interpretations belong to God?"* Joseph told them their end according to the dream, so the baker was hanged and the butler restored. Though Joseph had appealed to the butler to remember him, he forgot. We might well consider the Saviour's appeal to our mind to remember Him. Do we also forget?

When Pharaoh dreamed two dreams he could not interpret, the butler then remembered his fault and told the Pharaoh of Joseph. When Joseph was brought to Pharaoh, he again changed his coat. Now wearing the coat of a prophet, he revealed the meaning of Pharaoh's dreams and the things established by God, that God was going to bring to pass.

This was a coat such as the Lord Jesus wore in His death and resurrection. All the established purposes of God met in Him in the hour of His death. The essence of prophecy is the death of Christ and the subsequent resurrection. This testimony towers over time and causes John to explain that *"the testimony of Jesus is the spirit of prophecy"* (Rev. 19:10).

When Paul calls on Timothy not to be ashamed of that testimony, he reminds him that the essence of it was that the Saviour appeared to abolish death and bring life and immortality to light through this gospel. Joseph unfolded the need of the future to Pharaoh and the land of Egypt. But at Calvary Christ unfolded the need of the future to the whole world. In that way, when He went to the cross to die, He surely wore the Seer's coat. The future of every man, woman, boy, and girl ever born hung in the balance, and wearing such a coat He sealed that future for all believers as glorious.

To perpetuate the gospel that had its focal point in that glorious death, Paul was willing to be poured out as a drink offering on the sacrifice and service of the faith of those at Philippi, that they might rejoice together in the cause of Christ. That death showed Paul such a glorious future that for him to pour out everything to God was insignificant by comparison.

THE COAT OF THE SOVEREIGN

Then Joseph put on one last coat, the fine linen with a golden chain about his neck, exalted by the Pharaoh to be ruler over all of Egypt. Surely this points to the coat of exaltation that is the Lord's, entitling Him to *The Name*. Not a name, but The Name which indicates the majesty and presence of God. It is not at the Name of Jesus that all shall bow, terrestrial and celestial, and infernal, but at The Name given to Jesus—*The Name* with the rank, honor and dignity that is rightfully His, in view especially of the coats He wore.

Philippians 2:9-11, being introduced by *"Wherefore"* indicates that the exhortation to *"let this mind be in you"* refers to the mind that brought Him to the cross. But if we catch something of that mind, then we are carried beyond the cross to glory. That was the mind of Paul when he said he pressed toward the mark of the high calling of God in Christ Jesus. The calling is as high as the exalted Saviour Himself—the man Christ Jesus, who now has The Name.

—David B. Robins, July-August 1998, pp. 14-15,
and September-October 1998, pp. 8-9

52. THE GOD OF MEASURE

od has chosen to reveal Himself in various and wonderful ways, if by any means His creatures may discover who and what He is in all the wonders of His infinite being. One of those means of revealing Himself is by His great names and titles. Many of these are well-known to the Bible reader, but some are not so familiar. One of these lesser known titles is not shown in the KJV, but appears in 2 Corinthians 10:13 (JND). It is *"The God of Measure."* In many places in Scripture this aspect of God's character is borne out.

He is not an arbitrary God, doing things simply because He is almighty and sovereign. Behind His glorious works there are the eternal counsels (Isa. 46:10). Behind His mighty fiat there is the divine will, and behind all His dealings with humanity is His wondrous love. So that not only in the realms of angels, of suns and stars, of nations, or armies of heaven and of earth, but also in the lives of individuals, the God of Measure is especially at work.

• HE MEASURES THE TESTS OF LIFE (1 Cor. 10:13): *"God...will not suffer you to be tempted above that ye are able...to bear."* Testing is the common lot of all. We cannot escape it, but we can survive it. God has promised that every test will not exceed the measure of our ability to bear it. Even when it seems our limit has been reached and the "last straw" long ago covered up by more, the God of Measure has given us the assurance that, sore though it may be, it will not exceed His measure of our ability to bear it.

• HE MEASURES THE TRIVIA OF LIFE (Lk. 12:7): *"The hairs of your head are all numbered."* Now what possible significance to the Sovereign of the skies, the Lord of worlds, is the number of the hairs on our head? Not "counted," please note, but numbered! Every printer knows the difference between counting and numbering. To count 500 sheets of paper establishes how many there are. To number 500 sheets, each one has its own number. The lesson is clear that if God has numbered each hair of our heads, then we can be assured that there is not a detail of the body and its pains, the soul and its feelings, the spirit and its aspirations, that is unnoticed and measured by Him. What a comfort to those who bear heavy burdens for many years. He knows.

• HE MEASURES THE TEARS OF LIFE (Ps. 56:8): *"...Put Thou my tears into Thy bottle; are they not in Thy book?"* David knew about weeping. He had tears of sorrow in bereavement, tears of grief in his family; he had tears of remorse for his sin, tears of distress by his enemies. He wept tears in the home, tears in the wilderness, tears in the cave, tears in public, and tears in the secret place. Now in one of his nine "Golden" psalms, he reminds us that not one tear has fallen to the ground nor stained his pillow unnoticed by God. Not only does He notice our tears, and *that* we have wept, He records them in the Book of Tears *why* we have wept. And by divine chemistry He has gathered up the tears of the saints and deposited them in heaven's museum in His Bottle of Tears. There they will glisten in glory to the everlasting praise of *"the God of all comfort"* and in eternal remembrance of the One who wept for sinners and for their sorrows.

• HE MEASURES THE TRAVELLINGS OF LIFE (Ps. 56:8): *"Thou tellest [countest] my wanderings...."* When loved ones are away with many miles between, we count the days until they return. How ponderous do the hours of waiting seem for loved ones to come home. So with our God and our Father. When we wander from His fellowship, such is His loving heart, He yearns for our return. *"All day long"* He has waited for Israel. The prodigal's father pictures the waiting, longing, yearning heart of God looking for the wandering one. Amazing grace indeed it is that God counts the days of our wanderings until we return to His heart at last.

But there are things of God that *know no measure*. When it comes to His love, it *"passeth knowledge"* in every dimension of breadth and length and depth and height. The *"riches of His grace"* are *"manifold,"* *"abundant"* and *"multiplied."* As for His blessings, He has *"blessed us with all spiritual blessings in heavenly places in Christ."*

If we desire to enter into the divine Measuring Chamber by prayer and ask for the good things of God in the Counting House of His Treasures, we can rejoice in the assurance that the God of Measure is *"able to do exceeding abundantly above all that we ask or think, according to the power that worketh in us"* (Eph. 3:20).

—*J. Boyd Nicholson, Editorial, January-February 1994, p. 3*

53. Nest Among the Stars

I f Obadiah, the least among the Minor Prophets, has not had his due at the hands of students, the reasons are not far to seek. His subject is the disturbing one of judgment, and the judged are that tragic man and his descendants, who sought in vain for a place of repentance although sought carefully with tears.

The humanist cannot help feeling that Esau was rather badly treated and that that worm Jacob escaped too lightly. So in Obadiah's company we come face to face with the mystery of divine sovereignty, and those staggering words, *"Jacob have I loved, but Esau have I hated."* When all allowance has been made for the limitations of human language as a conveyance for divine ideas, the mystery remains to be a stone of stumbling, or an object of ingenious special pleading, or a foundation for a grim theological theory.

One of the advantages of being a humble Bible student unattached to any school is that, realizing the vastness of the subject and the smallness of the mind, it is permissible to dispense with theories on certain matters while preserving the firmest grasp on essential truth. How flat the round earth seems to dwellers of the Indian plains! We maintain our belief in the sovereignty of the eternal God to whom our tenses do not apply. No less do we maintain our belief in the awful responsibility of a man to decide the way his soul shall go.

The prophecy opens, *"The vision of Obadiah..."* He is a simple witness telling what he has seen. His brevity places his work in that class which comprises five miniature Scriptures: Philemon, 1 and 2 John, and Jude. War is declared against Edom; Esau's hour has come and although he hurls his challenge from the impregnable fortress which still stands to astonish the world, the armies of heaven have unfurled their banners and unsheathed their swords and there is to be no escape. The long day of grace has ended, the endless night of judgment has come. The nest among the stars is to be rifled, the cleft rock scaled, the vine left without a gleaning grape.

It was the due reward of his deeds; when Israel was plundered,

Edom approved. When foreigners entered into the city of the great king, the tongue of Esau added to the Babel sounds, speaking great swelling words. He shared the spoil of Jacob, and, manning the crossways to capture the fugitives and deliver them to their oppressors, disregarding the brotherly covenant.

But it was a short-lived triumph. With the measure they had meted it was measured to them again, pressed down and running over. For Israel, so fiercely, so righteously judged, there was mercy in store; although scattered like the chaff of the summer threshing floor, there was to be a gathering. Mount Seir, which is Petra, the poet's "rose-red city, half as old as time," the streets of the house of Jacob should possess all their possessions again, and the kingdom of Israel should be the kingdom of God.

While we wait for this fulfillment, we shall be wise if we learn again the old, old lesson of *"the nest among the stars."* It is a warning against the lust for leadership, the curse of hell and earth, of kingdoms and churches and homes. A variant is Adonijah's *"I will be king!"* It began with Satan and will only end with his overthrow.

"The pride of thine heart hat deceived thee, thou that dwellest in the clefts of the rock, whose habitation is high; that saith in his heart, 'Who shall bring me down to the ground?'" (v. 3). When shall we learn that before honor is humility? That we must take the lowest room if we would enjoy the highest place? Our faith has as its example He who had His nest among the stars by every right. Yet He was found in fashion as a man, saying, *"The foxes have holes, and the birds of the air have nests, but the Son of Man hath not where to lay His head"*—nowhere except a cross at last.

It was the proud eagle nature of Edom that was his downfall. Secure in his eyrie; strong to look the sun in the face; despising all lesser breeds; aiming at sovereignty for base ends he overstepped the boundary of mercy and it was true—

> *From the same cradle's side,*
> *From the same mother's knee*
> *One to long darkness and the frozen tide,*
> *One to the peaceful sea.* (Oliver Wendell Holmes)

For whom is the nest among the stars? By the grace of God it is for the worm of Jacob's line. They have seen the vision splendid, the way cast up on earth reaching to heaven, with the living God speaking His exceeding great and precious promises. In them all those promises are fulfilled, for the God of Abraham, Isaac and Jacob is their Father; His Son their Saviour; His Spirit their Indweller; His angels their servants; His book their wisdom; His heaven their home.

—A. C. Rose, November-December 1993, p. 12

54. REMEMBER! FORGET!

emember? At the end of a year we tend to engage in remembering the past. The trouble with some of us is: we remember what we should forget, and forget what we should remember.

Paul had it sorted out. He knew it was good and helpful to remember certain things in the past, but there were also things he wanted to forget.

"Call to remembrance the former days" (Heb. 10:32), says the writer to the Hebrews. Those were the early days of their salvation, when first the light of the gospel illuminated their hearts and they joyfully suffered loss for the Lord. It is good for us all to look back and to rejoice over that happy day.

> *O happy day, O happy day,*
> *When Jesus washed my sins away,*
> *He taught me how to watch and pray,*
> *And live rejoicing every day,*
> *Happy day, happy day,*
> *When Jesus washed my sins away.* (Philip Doddridge)

David also knew that there are some things good to remember. When he was *"in the wilderness,"* hunted for his life, he wrote, *"I have seen Thee in the sanctuary"* (Ps. 63:2). The remembrance of those holy moments in the past sustained him in his sorrow, and assured him that his soul would again be satisfied *"when I remember Thee"* (vv. 5-6).

So with us, when the way is hard and everything seems like *"a dry and thirsty land,"* we may reach the Fountainhead and drink deeply of refreshing memories of holy moments. Perhaps even at this moment we can recall a very special time at the Lord's Supper. Hearts were moved by God's Spirit, tears flowed as we remembered our beloved Lord in the giving of His sacred body and the shedding of His precious blood. A holy silence brooded over the saints and the light of the Lord's presence seemed to fill us with holy wonder and adoration. It is good to remember those moments in the sanctuary when the soul is dry and thirsty. They restore hope.

There is no occupation for the believing heart like remembering the Lord Jesus. This holy yet simple occupation calms the troubled mind, quietens the restless soul, clears the spiritual vision. Things are brought into focus and true values are established.

> *When to the cross I turn mine eye, and rest on Calvary,*
> *O Lamb of God, my sacrifice, I must remember Thee.*
> (James Montgomery)

Memory can be a blessed servant, but it can also be a cruel master. The recurring memory of past failure and sin can drive a child of God to distraction. If these have not been confessed to God, it is the work of the Holy Spirit to recall to us what has offended Him and to bring us by conviction to confession. But if the sins and failures have been honestly confessed to God, then His Word declares, *"He is faithful and just to forgive us our sins, and to cleanse us from all unrighteousness"* (1 Jn. 1:9).

We can be sure that when He forgives our sins, they are removed from the record—put out of His sight, behind His back, *"as far as the east is from the west"* and put out of His mind, to be remembered no more. We can lay down the burden of a troubled past under the precious blood of Christ, and leave it there. So we can holily and justly step into each new day with a clear sky between our souls and a faithful God, our holy and loving Father.

Paul reminds us that there were things to forget, (Phil. 3:13). He does not spell them out, but we may get a clue from his letter. In 2:30, he speaks of the Philippians' *"lack of service"* toward him. Perhaps when in prison in Caesarea they did not communicate with him. This failure of the saints towards him he wanted to forget.

How many lives have shrivelled up, nurturing bitterness over the failure of the saints towards them in the past—the things that should have been. The Jews would not eat *"the sinew that shrank."* Why? Because it would remind them of Jacob's failure (Gen. 32:32). What a bitter repast that is, picking the bones of the saints and chewing the fat over their failures. Forget it! Leave it with God!

Paul also wanted to forget things that might have been. What might Saul of Tarsus have been in Judaism if he had not met the Lord that day? Perhaps he would have reached the top in the hierarchy at Jerusalem. What might you have been today in the business world if you had not trusted Christ? Such speculations only breed frustration. Remember instead what God has made us in Christ!

Yes, let us remember the day of salvation, the days of the sanctuary, even the days of sorrow when the Lord drew near and went with us. Let us seek help and grace from God to put from our minds, once and for all, the forgiven sins and failures of the past—our own and others' against us, and above all—

> *This would I do, O Christ, my Lord,*
> *I would remember Thee!*
>   (James Montgomery)

—J. Boyd Nicholson, Editorial, November-December 1996, p. 3

55. The Upper Room Ministry

ohn 13–17 follow the conclusion of the Lord's public ministry as recorded in the Gospel according to John. Chapter 11, with the raising of Lazarus from the dead, brings the seven signs with their evangelical message to a close. John records, *"Many other signs truly did Jesus in the presence of His disciples which are not written in this book: but these are written that ye might believe that Jesus is the Christ, the Son of God; and that believing ye might have life through His name."*

Chapter 12, which follows, concludes with the announcement of His death and the increasing hatred and hostility of the Pharisees. The Lord says, *"Now is My soul troubled; and what shall I say? Father, save Me from this hour: but for this cause came I unto this hour."* Such is the dark background of hostility and foreboding that existed when the Lord drew His own aside to give them this precious, tender ministry in view of His imminent departure. From now on, with the exception of chapter 18, which records the crucifixion, all is in private with His own, and the nature of the Lord's ministry now changes accordingly.

The Upper Room Ministry can be summarized as follows:

Ch. 13: The Feet Washing—sanctification
Ch. 14: The Lord's Departure—consolation
Ch. 15: The Vine & the Branches—reproduction
Ch. 16: The Paraclete—instruction and conviction
Ch. 17: The Lord's Prayer—glorification

The Upper Room ministry provides an interesting comparison with the tabernacle in the Levitical economy. For example, when approaching the tabernacle, after passing through the gate, the first thing that was encountered was the bronze altar—the place of sacrifice. Continuing on, the priest came next to the laver at which he washed his hands and his feet—the place of cleansing. Making further progress, the priest entered the Holy Place, which was lit by the golden lampstand fed by the olive oil, and where fellowship with

God was possible as portrayed in the table of showbread. The priest then came to the veil, and beyond that lay the Holy of Holies, where none may enter except the high priest, and that only once a year, with incense, and the blood of the sin offering on the Great Day of Atonement. John 12 through 17 appears to take us on this priestly journey.

The Altar (Jn. 12): This chapter takes us to the altar of sacrifice. The Lord says, *"Except a corn of wheat fall into the ground and die, it abideth alone"* (v. 24). Again, *"Now is My soul troubled; and what shall I say? Father, save Me from this hour: but for this cause came I unto this hour."* And yet again, *"And I, if I be lifted up...will draw all men unto Me. This said He signifying by what death He should die."* The cross is clearly in view.

The Laver (Jn. 13): The Aaronic priest was completely washed at his consecration. Thereafter, he was only washed ceremonially at the laver, where he washed his hands prior to entering the Holy Place. It is suggested that John 13 takes us on to the laver. This was not a bathing all over, but of the hands and feet. It also did not involve blood or sacrifice. So the Lord reminds Peter, *"He that is* [bathed] *all over, needeth not save to wash his feet."* The laver is clearly in view, which speaks of the daily cleansing that we as believers must partake of, if we want to have have fellowship with God.

The Holy Place (Jn. 14-16): When the priest entered the Holy Place, the light of the golden candlestick fed by the pure olive oil was the sole means of illumination in that place. Without it, the beauties of that place would have been unseen. It is suggested that John 13–16 finds us in the Holy Place. The Lord emphasizes the illuminating work of the Spirit, and the fellowship that the disciples would enjoy through the Spirit.

The Holy of Holies (Jn. 17): Beyond the Holy Place, behind the veil, lay the Holy of Holies—the very dwelling place of God, amid the cherubim. John 17 takes us beyond the veil, and into the Holy of Holies itself. What a privilege for mortals like ourselves to listen in to an intimate conversation between the Father and the Son. We stand in awe as we hear about the Eternities, and about all that had pertained before the world was. We are amazed to learn that we also are part of that conversation, that we are mentioned in this prayer to His Father, and that His desires for us will not be denied—that where He is, there we too shall be, to behold His glory, the glory that He had with the Father before the world was.

—W. H. Burnett, January-February 1999, p. 10

56. The Silent Plumb Line

is hands were strong, but there was an artistry about them that interested me as a lad. My paternal grandfather had learned the trade of the stone mason. While that activity as an occupation had been left far behind, he still loved to work with stone.

A well-placed blow with the mallet and chisel would split a piece of stone exactly as he wanted it, exposing the beauty of color or grain. Then, piece by piece, he would build a wall, the stones being fitted together in such a way that no mortar was needed to hold or strengthen it.

There was one simple piece of equipment, however, that was frequently used; he was never without it. It was the plumb line. Everything had to be "plumb." That piece of cord with its lead weight was the rule, the standard, the point of reference. It was not dependent on any of the stones nor influenced by the approval of the onlooker. It was always consistent. It could not be disputed nor adjusted. It hung, always silent, but indicating what was right, and would therefore remain. What was "out of plumb" would be removed.

The value of the plumb line is in its ability to show the correctness of the vertical measure. It is this that affects stability and strength. So much in the world and in Christendom these days is addicted to horizontal growth. Some measure "church growth" by increased numbers. That is horizontal growth. However, the Lord is first interested in the vertical development of His people. If this is not according to the "plumb line" then the horizontal work will be "out of plumb," unstable and unacceptable.

That vertical growth upwards is the purpose of the spiritual gifts in Ephesians 4, that, *"speaking the truth in love [we] may grow up into Him in all things"* (v. 15). As the body is being built up, the plumb line of the truth makes sure that the growth is *"into Him...the head, even Christ."*

Vertical growth downward is the result of Christ dwelling (feeling at home) in the believer's hearts, *"being rooted and grounded in love"* (Eph. 3:17). The strengthening of the foundation—well *"grounded"*—and the lengthening of the tap root is governed by the plumb line of the love of Christ.

This must be the aim of the child of God personally, and of the shepherds for the church collectively in the matter of growth. It must be growing up into Christ and rooted and grounded in love.

The third vision of Amos was that of the Lord standing on a wall that had been built according to the plumb line (Amos 7:7). Now the Lord was going to set the plumb line *"in the midst of My people Israel"* (v. 8). Special relationship involves special responsibility. The nations around were one thing, but Israel was His people; and there, right *"in the midst"* was the silent witness of God's holy standard by which they were continually measured.

So it is with the assembly. Paul warns those who would build that they *"take heed" **how** they build. Christ Himself is the standard. While His Person, His work, and His doctrine may be distinguished, they can never be separated, and it is on this foundation that the building stands. The plumb line is set *"in the midst."* Silently and continually it is the divine test of what will stand and what will not.

Peter points back to the promise in Isaiah 28:16 (1 Pet. 2:6) and links it to the Church built with living stones. The Lord tells Isaiah that He will use His plumb line, and by the holy standards of His righteousness He will test the building. He speaks there of a solemn thing He calls *"the refuge of lies."*

Wherever men or women seek to protect themselves or vindicate their actions in that wretched refuge of lies, they are to be assured the silent plumb line of truth will be applied. Their darling projects of fabrication and falsehood will be swept away; they will be exposed at last and their hiding place destroyed (Isa. 28:17).

The plumb line points to another day when the Master Builder will test everyone's work. It will not be the size of the work, nor the apparent success of our efforts. Our work will be measured as to what *"sort"* it is. How we built and what we built will be tested.

The plumb line is the divine test that proves if what we have built is *"according to truth."* The fire will test what materials we have built with—according to the abiding values of eternity or the disintegrating values of time. Let us each solemnly remember the Lord's words to Amos: *"I will set a plumb line in the midst of My people."*

—*J. Boyd Nicholson, Editorial, March-April 1995, p. 3*

57. The Mystery of Suffering

t is a great honor to be able to look at the divine workings in a soul while in the crucible of suffering. The book of Job does this in a most vivid way. It teaches lessons about the error of forming conclusions as to the "why" of the calamities of others. The book of Job shows the folly of the carnal view of suffering. God did not explain to Job the reason why, so how could his friends have an answer?

Satan's activities are unmasked here in a way not given elsewhere. He marches as a conqueror greedy of spoil (1:7; 2:2). See Habakkuk 1:6 for the same word. He has no love for the child of God. The evil one is dedicated to the destruction of the saints. He is revealed as a liar, maligning both God and His servant, and a coward.

The attitude of the three friends could be summed up as follows:

ELIPHAZ: He represents the idea that this one tragic experience is an adequate basis of knowledge from which to answer Job's problem. He lacks authority, however, and has no power to solve the spiritual dilemma.

His approach only produces arguments, but all experience has to be tested by God's Word. Eliphaz represents the existentialism of the patriarch's time, not unlike that of today.

BILDAD: He represents the tradition of the fathers (8:8), but it requires more than the traditional approach to speak for God and reach a human heart that is breaking under the vexing question, "Why?"

ZOPHAR: He represents the law and religion (11:6, 14). This approach, though clear as the moon, is equally as cold. It cannot bring the sufferer into the presence of God. The thoughts of those three are basically similar. "How can Job be righteous and suffer like this?" In the light of the New Testament we can say, "How can he be a son and not suffer?" (see Heb. 12:5-11).

The contributions of the three only evoke from Job frustration and self-vindication. He is outraged at their accusations, and they cannot refute his reasoning, but they provoke him to have wrong conclusions as to God's intentions, and incite him to affirm his own right-eousness at all costs (27:5).

Chapters 29–31 contain some 180 references of Job to himself in one way or another. In Chapter 29, it is the "I" of *prosperity* in the past; in chapter 30, it is the "I" of *adversity* in the present; in chapter 31, it is the "I" of *innocence* resulting in false confidence.

ELIHU: This one's ministry is different and has a spiritual approach (32:4, 8, 11-14, 21). He uses grace and truth (33:3, 7, 8-17). He understands that God's dealings are not always punitive, but often are corrective and instructive. He insists that God is truly just (34:10, 12, 17, 19, 23, 31; also 36:10, 22). He concludes by suggesting that trust in God is better than trying to unravel and explain the enigmas of life (37:23-24).

When God speaks at last, what a revelation of the grandeur and glory of the Sovereign Creator. God speaks of the universe, the animals, birds, and mankind. God said to Job, "Gird yourself like a strong (*geber,* Heb.) man, not the frail mortal man (*enosh,* Heb.), and give Me an answer." Job had said quite a few things that he would do and say if only he could be near enough to God! In view of God's greatness and glory, Job acknowledges his own puny size, and repents in dust and ashes.

Previously Job had been concerned about the eyes that saw him, but now his eyes see God, and then all is so different. This is the true source of grace and humility (Isa. 6). What lovely grace is seen in Job as he prays for those who had caused him such added grief! God knew His servant and in spite of Satan's calumny, God proved Satan to be wrong.

The latter end of Job is beautiful. No wonder it concludes with Job dying *"satisfied"* with days. It was all so worthwhile. Such are the wonderful ways of God. No one teaches as He does.

There is much confusion in the minds of many of God's dear people regarding suffering. Some feel that, as a child of God, it should never come their way. Others believe that God *causes* everything. However, what He *causes* is one thing, what He *permits* is altogether another.

Let us never forget that we are living in a world damaged and distorted through sin, full of human error. God does not violate the human will and its decisions, but He often does providentially over-rule them for good (Gen. 50:20). We only see the *"now"* with very limited vision, but He sees the *"afterward"* with total knowledge. Let us trust Him in the dark, and keep on praying even in the dark, remembering the promises of Psalm 97:11; 112:4; Isaiah 50:10; Romans 8:28; and James 1:12.

There will be an *"afterward"*—*"the end of the Lord"*—if not here, then in the glory.

—*B. D. Goatley, September-October 1995, p. 9*

58. Taffy

affy is the nickname for a Welshman. I have known a few Taffys along the way, but one stands out in my memory.

We met in an Air Force canteen in London during World War II. I had left the noise and smoke of the tearoom area to find a quiet spot alone on a stairway to drink my mug of hot tea. It wasn't long till my quiet was interrupted by another airman wanting to know if he could sit there with me. He was, I judged, about ten years older than I and looked pale and unwell. "I'm Taffy," he said, sitting down. I could tell by the white flash in his cap that he too was on air crew training. As it turned out, we were both waiting for a posting to Initial Wing any day.

"I think we should stick together," he said. His farewell from the previous unit had involved some heavy drinking. Up until then, he had never tasted alcohol and the results were gastronomically devastating, crowned with a thundering headache and a smiting conscience. It was an opportunity, of course, to tell him about the Saviour.

He sat quietly listening. Then with bowed head and downcast eyes, he told me he knew the gospel. His mother was a praying Christian.

As far as "sticking together," we had little choice in the matter. Men were being shipped all over the country, even overseas. But when the postings came through, there were our names on the same list, posted to the same town in England.

Newquay was a beautiful resort on the Cornwall coast where the Air Force had taken over the hotels along the seafront to accommodate the men. The hotels had been suitably stripped to the boards for our basic comfort.

Well, we were in the same town. That was something. There we were lined up at the railway station according to which hotel we were being sent. Yes! there we were, put in the same flight, going to the same hotel! Of course, by now I was convinced the Lord was at work; this was confirmed when we were assigned the same room—just the two of us!

The Welsh love to sing. Taffy had a rich baritone voice and in the evenings often would lie on his bunk and regale my Scottish ear with some of his country's beautiful songs. One of these, all in Welsh, was about a field of daffodils. I heard it so often I learned the strange sounding words.

Taffy failed the course and halfway through was posted to another unit. We had become good friends and we lay on our bunks much of the last night he was there, talking about the things of God and eternity. It was war and young men were dying; I was deeply concerned about his eternal soul. I appealed to him to trust the Saviour, but his quiet response was, "Yes, Boyd, I will...someday."

Years of war ground on and regularly Taffy was prayed for. One day while flying, I became deeply concerned about him. I had no idea where he had gone or if he was even still alive. If I had remembered his address, I could have written him, but it was a Welsh address with unusual names. So I asked the Lord to return his address to my memory. Before I landed, the complete details came back to me. Indeed to this day I have not forgotten that address!

I wrote him at once to discover he had married and his home was now in Birmingham in the Midlands. Try as I might, I never did get to see him.

The war ended. Twenty-five years later, I was visiting the UK from Canada and found myself in Birmingham. I remembered that Taffy lived there. I searched the phone book and discovered among many with the same name, one that had his initials. I phoned and the greeting on the other end was unmistakably a son of Wales! I spoke without divulging my identity and began by quoting the words of the Welsh song of the daffodils from Newquay days. "Boyd! Where are you?" He almost leapt into the phone.

We were only five minutes away and soon at the door. There he was, the same, yet like us all, a bit older. The visit was wonderful, but there was one question I was waiting to ask. Had he ever trusted the Saviour? "No, not yet, but I will...someday."

Another dozen years rolled by, and Taffy was not forgotten at the Throne of Grace. Again we were back near Birmingham. Without any advance notice, we located his new address and went to the door unannounced. He opened the door and after a joyous greeting, I asked him, "Well, Taffy, God has spared you these many years. What about it now?"

"Yes, Boyd, at last, I'm saved and on the way to heaven!" What joy! What thanksgiving to the God who had heard a mother's prayers and would not let her boy go. Shortly after, he died of a heart attack. Oh, what mercy his *some day* wasn't too late!

Praying these many years for a loved one? Faint not! Remember Taffy...and all those years.

—*J. Boyd Nicholson, Editorial, November-December 1994, p. 3*

59. MOSES, THE MAN OF GOD

Ask a Jew. Ask a Christian. Ask a Muslim. They will all give the same answer: Moses was a mighty man of God. Moses was a prophet indeed. Turn to the Jew again and ask why his people still revere the name of Moses more than 3,000 years after his death. There are many reasons. Was not Moses the man who first gave them in written form a history of the early days of the Jewish race? And was not Moses himself a key figure in that history?

It was Moses likewise who first gave them a sense of national cohesion when he challenged the powerful Pharaoh and secured their freedom. He had found them in abject misery as slaves, even threatened with extinction, and then rescued them from the rigors of Egypt for a new life in Canaan. At the same time he drew them away from the idol gods of Egypt and called them back to the God of their fathers, with fresh revelations of Jehovah's name and nature.

Once free of Egypt, he marched them to the Mount Sinai region where he *"brought forth the people out of the camp to meet with God"* (Ex. 19:17). It was there that Moses received from Jehovah's hand a body of laws for the new-born nation. Those laws he then codified and presented to the people for their guidance in every area of life: personal, social and national. If Abraham was their father as a race, Moses was no less their father as a nation. And what a nation!

But much more important than the opinion of any Jew, Christian, or Muslim is the divine appraisal of Moses. *"There arose not a prophet since in Israel like unto Moses, whom the Lord knew face to face"* (Deut. 34:10). Written at the end of Moses' life, these words mean much more than the customary speaking well of the dead. Years before, when Moses' credentials were being questioned by his own family, the Lord intervened in a most emphatic way: *"If there be a prophet among you, I...will speak unto him in a dream. My servant Moses is not so...With him will I speak mouth to mouth...and the similitude of the Lord shall he behold"* (Num. 12:6-8).

"Mouth to mouth" and *"face to face"*—these are staggering

words when viewed in the context of Scripture as a whole. On the one hand, we see a mere mortal, the author of Psalm 90 with its emphasis on the frailty of man and the brevity of life; on the other hand, we have the eternal God, the Creator of the universe, *"the blessed and only Potentate...dwelling in the light which no man can approach unto."* Yet Moses was able, by divine invitation, to enter the tabernacle in the wilderness and commune with the Almighty. *"When Moses was gone into the tabernacle of the congregation to speak with Him, he heard the voice of One speaking unto him"* (Num. 7:89). Again, *"he heard the voice of One speaking unto him from off the mercy seat that was upon the ark of the testimony, from between the two cherubims"* (Num. 7:89).

When the law was given at Mount Sinai amid dreadful thunders and lightnings, only a select few were allowed even to approach the mount, but: *"Moses alone shall come near the Lord."* A privileged man indeed! And who but Moses could have foreseen the coming of Christ and presumed to say, *"A prophet shall the Lord raise up of your brethren like unto me"*? This might appear as conceit on the part of Moses, but it was a prophetic utterance based on a divine revelation. Of all the Old Testament worthies who prefigured Christ, Moses alone seemed to be aware of that fact.

The Lord Jesus reminded the Jews of Moses' prophecy: *"Had ye believed Moses, ye would have believed Me; for he wrote of Me."* Peter also quoted those words of Moses in one of his post-Pentecost sermons, and insisted that Christ was indeed *"that Prophet"* (Acts 3:22-23). Stephen likewise used the same passage to convince his bloodthirsty hearers that in crucifying Jesus of Nazareth they had murdered their Messiah, the One Moses had both predicted and prefigured (Acts 7:37).

Later prophets in Israel continually referred the people back to Moses and his writings; indeed his name is mentioned after his death more than any other Old Testament character. It was also from the writings of Moses that the blessed Lord quoted when tempted by Satan. Then in resurrection life He explained the Old Testament prophecies, *"beginning at Moses."*

Thus Moses stands without peer among the Hebrew prophets. But Moses was not just a prophet; he was a man of many parts. He was an outstanding *historian*, more than a thousand years before Herodotus, the so-called "father of history." And the writings of Moses are much more than a record of events. They stress moral and spiritual values, carrying an overlay of prophetic teaching as well.

Moses also stands out as a *lawgiver*: *"the law was given by Moses."* History speaks of other famous lawgivers: Solon, for example, one of the Seven Wise Men of Greece. But he too lived centuries after Moses, and his laws were based solely on human wisdom, whereas those of Moses were of divine origin, revealing God's mind and character.

By any standard Moses was an acknowledged leader among men. It was no mean task to take some two million unorganized and spiritless serfs, weld them together as one, and then lead them to victory against one of the world's greatest powers.

For this position, the Lord had trained His servant in two very different schools: first by his princely upbringing in the Egyptian palace where he was exposed to administrative processes and court protocol, and where he received a liberal education, which was later reflected in his writings; then in the desert, as a shepherd amid harsh conditions, he learned lasting lessons in patience and labors which brought little thanks or reward. Never say that Moses had to unlearn in the desert *all* he learned in Egypt. Both schools were necessary.

Scripture also refers to Moses as a *priest* (Ps. 99:6), not in the official sense like Aaron, but as the man who represented the people before God, even when Aaron failed. Thus he prefigured the Lord as both prophet and priest (Heb. 3:1). Indeed much of his time after the Exodus was spent in teaching on the one hand and beseeching on the other—teaching the law of the Lord, and then beseeching Him for mercy when the people broke those laws.

On the human level, he had represented the people before the King of Egypt, but on a higher level, before the King of Glory. It was here he excelled as an *intercessor*, a true type of the One who *"ever liveth to make intercession for us."* Centuries later the name of Moses was recalled with that of Samuel as men who interceded with God for His erring people (Jer. 15:1). Standing before God on behalf of others is one of the highest in human experience.

Concerning intercession, one of the early Puritan writers once listed some of the marvels it had wrought: it had unlocked prison doors; it had made the grave yield up its dead; it had opened and shut heaven; it had stayed the sun's chariot in the skies. And then, "that which surpasseth all else, it hath taken hold of the Almighty Himself, when on His full march against some particular person or people, and hath put Him to a merciful retreat." *"This was that Moses..."*—the man of God.

—W. P. W. McVey, September-October 1996, pp. 8-9

60. A Bucket of Joy

I n the more than forty years I knew him, I never saw him lose the joy of his salvation. Give him an eighth of an inch of opportunity and he was ready to tell you how he was saved. (Dare I say I heard it a thousand times and knew what was coming next?) He'd tell how his knees smote each other in the gallery of the old Massey Hall in Toronto when the gospel penetrated his conscience as a young man and he came under the conviction of the Holy Spirit about his sins. He relived with joy that first night in Christ, lying on his bed and singing:

> *"My old companions, fare ye well,*
> *I will not go with you to hell,*
> *I mean with Jesus Christ to dwell,*
> *I will go, I will go."* (Richard Jukes)

It doesn't mean he had never wept, nor passed through deep waters. But there was always that abiding joy in the God of his salvation that irradiated his countenance and disarmed the stranger. It made him easy to talk to, or perhaps more often, to listen to, as he so readily and inoffensively gave an answer to any who wondered about the quality of his hope and the reality of his faith.

When he was more than 90 years old, he was sitting on a bench in one of our shopping malls, resting a few minutes and enjoying watching the people go by. A young lady came out of a store, took her place at the other end of the bench, and began to unfold her lunch package. When all was set out and ready, she fumbled in her oversize handbag and pulled out some cigarettes. She put one in her mouth, got out her lighter, struck the flint and was about to ignite the thing, when she was suddenly aware of the old gentleman on the other end of the bench who was watching the procedure with interest. "Oh, sorry, sir," she volunteered, "You don't mind if I smoke, do you?"

"No, no," came the gentle reply, "I don't mind at all—so long as you're not a Christian." The light flickered in the air, the weed trembled on her lips. "You know what a Christian is, don't you, m'dear?" said the old gentleman kindly.

"Well...er, yes, I think so," she faltered.

"Well now, just let me tell you all about it..." and away he went, eyes sparkling. With evident delight, he told yet another precious soul about the secret of his joy.

A few days before he went home to be with the Lord, in his 96th year, he was taken into the emergency ward of our hospital. While the nurse was plugging him into the support equipment, he was doing his best to plug her into the gospel.

Joy! Have we lost it? It seems many have. Oh, yes, on the way to heaven, and sure of it, but not really enjoying the journey.

With the departure of joy, strength diminishes, for *"the joy of the Lord is your strength"* (Neh. 8:10).

With the departure of joy, satisfaction is dissipated, for it is with the bucket of joy that we draw refreshment from the wells of salvation (Isa. 12:3). When joy is gone, service is affected. David discovered that his teaching, his testimony, and his worship had all been affected with the departure of his joy.

The lost souls around us do not need tidy packages of limpid lectures, as clear as the moonlight and just as cold. They have never in their lives tasted one moment of pure joy. Joy is fruit from the Holy Spirit and they cannot know it. Happiness on occasions they may have; pleasure they may taste for a season, but never joy.

David not only lost his own joy, he lost the ability to enjoy other people's joy: *"Make me to hear joy and gladness,"* he prayed (Ps. 51:8).

What do the lost around us see in us? Just another human burdened with the cares of this life, concerned about the same things as they? Or do they see something else? They may not identify it, but they ought to be able to see something of the radiance of Christ in us, our hope of glory, and feel free to ask us the reason for that hope.

But how does it happen? We know there is no "switch" to turn it on. From where does that joy come? Well, we know it is of the Spirit of God, but we may contribute to it. There is joy in serving the Lord (Ps. 100:2). We don't wait until we "feel like it;" do it, and the joy will come. There is joy in feeding on the Word. Jeremiah tells us,

"Thy Word was unto me the joy and rejoicing of mine heart." There is joy in recalling the goodness of God to us. May God help us to show to poor perishing souls around that it is a wonderful thing to be saved.

Well, the old soldier has confirmed the words of David's Messianic 16th Psalm, *"In Thy presence is fullness of joy,"* and I doubt not that with holy laughter he has recounted there, amidst the holy blest, the wonderful story of God's grace to him.

He was my beloved father-in-law, and I thank God I was privileged to see and share his joy.

—*J. Boyd Nicholson, Editorial, July-August 1994, p. 3*

61. The Patience of Christ

he Lord direct your hearts into the love of God, and into the patience of Christ" (2 Thess. 3:5, RV). The expression, "the patience of Christ," could possibly be interpreted in three ways. First, it could mean that we may be patient in all our sufferings as Christ was in His (Heb. 12:2). Or that since Christ is expecting till His enemies be made the footstool of His feet (Heb. 10:13), so should we be patient in our hope of His triumph and our complete deliverance.

But the text could be rendered, "The Lord teach and enable you to love as God loves, and to be patient as Christ is patient." The word for patient is *hupomone*, literally, "an abiding under," signifying the need of abiding patience under all circumstances of life.

Thoughts about our Lord's patience encourage us, so let us ask, what is He waiting for?

THE DAY OF REUNION

It is almost 2000 years since His promise of John 14:3. Has He forgotten? Could He? Never! The consummation of this event (described in 1 Thess. 4:17; Eph. 5:27; Jn. 17:24 and Rev. 19:7) is constantly the patient, steadfast expectation of Christ. Surely we can be patient as He is, for this glorious, yet soon coming event—perhaps today.

THE DAY OF HIS REWARDS

The day of His rewards is described by various expressions: *"the day of Christ"* (Phil. 2:16); *"the day of Jesus Christ"* (Phil. 1:6); *"the day of the Lord Jesus"* (1 Cor. 5:5); *"the Day"* (1 Cor. 3:13); and *"that Day"* (2 Tim. 1:12, 18; 4:8).

We know He is waiting for the day when He will reward His servants. The rewards? Just a glimpse of 1 Corinthians 9:25, 2 Timothy 4:8, James 1:12, 1 Peter 5:4 and Revelation 2:10 is sufficient proof for our hearts to be encouraged to plod on in patient, steadfast service until He comes.

THE DAY OF HIS POWER

Read Psalm 110:1 and realize that while the enemies of our Lord are at present ruling in power over the earth, yet He is patiently waiting until the Father consummates this promise. The complete destruction of all His enemies is recorded in 2 Thessalonians 1:3-10, 2 Thessalonians 2:5-9, Psalm 2:4-9, and Revelation 6:17.

THE DAY OF HIS MILLENNIAL GLORY

A threefold distinction of this glory is indicated: with *the Church* in Revelation 21; with *Israel* in Ezekiel 37:1-14, Zechariah 12:10 and 13:2, and Romans 11:26; and with *the nations* in Zechariah 9:10, 14:9 and Isaiah 2.

Many Old Testament prophecies abundantly tell of that coming glory which will be on the earth during His millennial reign. How patient He is!

THE DAY OF THE NEW CREATION

God's eternal purpose is recorded in Ephesians 1:10 that *"He might gather together in one all things in Christ, both which are in heaven, and which are on earth; even in Him"* (see Col. 1:20; Rev. 21:1-5). Blessed new creation, when sin shall be no more! This is part of the great work of His patience. His steadfast longing and waiting for the fulfillment of the purposes of God put our hearts to shame as we consider our need of *"the patience of Christ."*

> *I am waiting for the dawning*
> *Of the bright and blessed day,*
> *When the darksome night of sorrow*
> *Shall have vanished far away;*
> *When forever with the Saviour,*
> *Far beyond this vale of tears,*
> *I shall swell the song of worship*
> *Through the everlasting years.*

I am waiting for the coming
Of the Lord who died for me;
O His words have thrilled my spirit,
"I will come again for thee."
I can almost hear His footfall
On the threshold of the door,
And my heart, my heart is longing
To be with Him evermore.   (S. Trevor Francis)

—John W. Bramhall, November-December 1996, p. 16

62. HE SHALL REIGN

he first direct question in the Old Testament was asked of a troubled man, *"Where art thou?"* when Adam vainly tried to hide from God. The first direct question in the New Testament was asked of a troubled king, *"Where is He...?"* It was asked concerning the newborn King of the Jews.

To Adam as he awakened to life, God said, *"Have dominion."* Adam was set over all creation. For a time, in innocence, he was king of the earth, a dominion many have lusted after.

Sadly, this king abdicated his throne and went into hiding! Deposed by sin, stripped of his radiant garment, his crown in the dust, and concealing himself with his consort Eve among the trees of the garden, he had wilfully yielded his dominion to Satan, the enemy of God and man. However, this wicked usurper did not become the king of the earth but the god of this world.

The history of kings fills the libraries of men, but none was born already a king. That is the singular glory of the Lord from heaven, the Son of God.

Darkness fell upon God's earthly people, and heaven was silent for four hundred years after Malachi laid down his pen. Many a longing eye must have looked for deliverance and many a broken heart must have cried for a saviour, a mighty deliverer, who would come in power and fulfill the words of the prophets.

At last, there came an angel to the virgin Mary with the message of God's King:

> *He shall be great, and shall be called the Son of the Highest: and the Lord God shall give unto Him the throne of His father David: and He shall reign over the house of Jacob for ever; and of His kingdom there shall be no end* (Lk. 1:32-33).

God the Father gave Him; great angels announced Him, the heavenly host praised God at His arrival; the stars of heaven pointed to Him; the prophets foretold Him; the Scriptures declared Him; the rich and the poor worshiped before Him. As a King, He has no peer.

His claim to the throne of David was legitimate; His authority was evident; and His power and wisdom were unsurpassed.

A Potentate with such authority and power might well strike fear into the hearts of His subjects, but His decree is "Peace," His banner is "Love," and "Compassion" is the beating of His heart. "Righteousness" is His rule and "Holiness" His character.

No conscript service will He demand of His people: *"His yoke is easy."* No grievous taxation does He lay upon His subjects: *"His burden is light."* His riches are unbounded and His treasuries are open.

He came to heal the broken-hearted; to bring the wealth of heaven to the poor; to give sight to the blind; to offer deliverance to the captives; and to set at liberty those crushed by the calamities of life. More than dealing with social ills and physical problems, He came to deal with the root cause of the whole moral and spiritual disorder. He was not only born a King, He was also born a Saviour from sin.

Oh, what a Visitor to this vale of tears! Angels might well envy the sons of men. How the weary inhabitants of earth would welcome Him—but did they? He was born a King, but those who should have been His willing subjects mocked His claims. He was crowned with thorns, anointed with spittle, and the royal scarlet He wore was drawn from His bleeding back with the lash. At last they took Him out to the only throne men ever gave Him, and they nailed Him to it through His blessed hands and feet.

Be not deceived, beneath that thorny crown lay all the authority of Godhood. Only a thought, a single word from those parched lips and the earth would have opened up beneath the feet of His tormentors. One word and a battalion of over seventy thousand eager angels would have sped from heaven to destroy this world and its wretched inhabitants. He speaks from the cross. What is it that He says? *"Father, forgive them, they know not what they do."* Oh, what kind of wondrous love is this!

He was born a King and He died a King. When this old world sees Him again, He will still be a King. Not robed in the homespun of a carpenter, speaking "Peace" but blazing in majesty and leading the armies of heaven to judge, make war and deal with His enemies.

Who are the enemies of this King of all kings? *"Them that know not God, and that obey not the gospel of our Lord Jesus Christ"* (2 Thess. 1:8).

Dear reader, have you obeyed the gospel and received this wondrous Saviour as your own? If not, quickly bow the knee!

> *One day the trumpet will sound for His coming,*
> *One day the skies with His glory will shine;*
> *Wonderful day, my beloved ones bringing;*
> *Glorious Saviour, this Jesus is mine!*
> *Living, He loved me; dying, He saved me;*
> *Buried, He carried my sins far away;*
> *Rising, He justified freely forever:*
> *One day He's coming–oh glorious day!*
>
> (J. Wilbur Chapman)

—J. Boyd Nicholson, Editorial, November-December 1997, p. 3

63. DIVINE AUTHORITY OR HUMAN OPINION?

hen a public figure was lecturing on the need to restore values to our culture, a college student asked him, "On what do you build your values?" The speaker was flustered. He looked down and said, "I don't know."

That's just the trouble. He had no authority. Modern man desperately needs what this man lacked—a firm foundation on which to base his judgments. He needs an infallible standard to guide him in all matters of faith and morals.

God has provided such an infallible authority in His Word, the Bible. This wonderful book provides the basis for sound judgments and wise decisions. The Bible is absolute truth. Jesus said, *"Thy Word is truth."* There is no risk in following its teachings, no fear it will change from day to day.

The alternative to divine authority is human opinion. "The Bible says…" is replaced by "I think…" Fact gives way to feeling. There are no more absolutes; everything is relative.

We know too well that there is no uniformity to human opinion. There is an endless variety of viewpoints, each clamoring to be heard. The result is confusion and chaos. When human opinion rules, there is no way of deciding whose opinion is right. One person's opinion is no better (or worse) than another's.

If God's Word is rejected and opinion takes its place, the natural tendency is for man's word to conflict with God's. This explains the downward moral drift we witness today.

God has given various authoritative laws to govern human behavior. Here are some basic ones:

- God is to be loved with all the heart, soul, mind, and strength;
- He is to be acknowledged as the Creator;
- human life is sacred, the marriage relationship is sacred, and the family unit is sacred;
- man is given the place of headship in the human chain of command;
- immorality is forbidden;

- children are to respect their parents;
- human governments are to be obeyed.

Man refuses to bow to these divine principles. What happens when a society abandons the authority of God whether found in the sacred Scriptures or written in the hearts of all mankind? What happens when human opinion takes over?

People give themselves over to all forms of immorality. Marriage is scorned in favor of a live-in relationship formerly called fornication or adultery. Sodomites are accepted as respectable members of the race, and the homosexual lifestyle is legalized. Even homosexual marriages are recognized by the state. Residual laws against incest are unenforced. Without absolute standards, any form of sexual disorder is approved, even glamorized. After all, isn't it popular opinion that counts?

The family unit largely disappears as a stabilizing influence in the community. Public sentiment favors divorce for any reason. Latchkey kids are raised by single parents. Respect for parents disappears, in fact, disrespect is dramatized on TV. Children can get a divorce from their parents.

Man's headship in the home ends. The buck no longer stops with him. Radical feminism demands equal authority and gets it.

Violence becomes so widespread that the government is unable to cope. Thefts, rapes, terrorism, tortures, and murders hardly make it into the newspapers. The average citizen is shocked by the brutality in the daily news, so much so that he is afraid to open his door. Politicians promise peace and security but fail to deliver. People come to despise their rulers and speak evil of them. The breakdown of law and order causes the populace to look for a dictator, a superman to solve the problems by inaugurating a new world order.

Materialism is the name of the game in business. Men are lovers of money, and success is gauged by the extent of their possessions. Greed rules out any semblance of ethics. In a cutthroat society, honesty becomes a synonym for bankruptcy. He who dies with the most toys wins.

The names of God and Christ are banned from government, school, and all public life. Secular humanism becomes the prevailing religion. Man trumpets his own achievements. What can he not do? He is invincible. Bookstores feature an endless variety of titles on self-love. William Henley's blasphemous poem, *Invictus*, becomes the national anthem.

> *Out of the night that covers me*
> *Black as the pit from pole to pole.*
> *I thank whatever gods may be,*
> *For my unconquerable soul.*

> *In the fell clutch of circumstance,*
> *I have not winced nor cried aloud.*
> *Under the bludgeonings of chance.*
> *My head is bloody but unbowed.*

> *Beyond this place of wrath and tears,*
> *Looms but the horror of the shade;*
> *And yet the menace of the years,*
> *Finds and shall find me unafraid.*

> *It matters not how strait the gate,*
> *How charged with punishment the scroll,*
> *I am the master of my fate,*
> *I am the captain of my soul.*

Christians, however, are singing different words. They have the national anthem of another kingdom.

> *Out of the light that dazzles me,*
> *Bright as the sun from pole to pole,*
> *I thank the God I know to be,*
> *For Christ the conqueror of my soul.*

> *Since His the sway of circumstance,*
> *I would not wince nor cry aloud.*
> *Under that rule which men call chance,*
> *My head with joy is humbly bowed.*

> *Beyond this place of sin and tears,*
> *That life with Him! and His the aid*
> *That, spite the menace of the years,*
> *Keeps and shall keep me unafraid.*

I have no fear though strait the gate,
He cleared from punishment the scroll;
Christ is the Master of my fate,
Christ is the Captain of my soul.
　　　—*My Captain* by Dorothy Day

As a result of this failure to conform to the world, there is increasing hostility toward Christ and His followers. Because men are despisers of good, they vent their rage against Christianity. This opposition includes ridicule, insults, reviling, blasphemies, legal restraints, physical attacks, and even martyrdoms. The anti-Christian spirit finds its culmination in an antichrist.

People turn to the occult, to eastern mysticism, to New Age philosophies, and to the freedom these religions offer them. They have a multiplicity of cults to choose from. False prophets promise prosperity in an age of apostasy. Some claim to be the Messiah and people are duped.

The disintegration of society sees a population without natural affection, a people given over to selfish pleasure. Men are unloving, unfaithful, and unthankful. Life is cheap; abortuaries murder millions of the unborn—an unprecedented holocaust, yet quietly accepted by most. In some places old folks are put to sleep and "doctors" assist suicides.

No wonder the Bible says, *"Where there is no revelation, the people cast off restraint"* (Prov. 29:18, NKJV). This means that when God and His Word are not recognized and obeyed, men abandon themselves to unbridled evil. Civilization returns to jungle life, Everyone does what is right in his own eyes. We see it all around us today. Even people without any particular love for the Bible are alarmed. They can see that our culture is on a toboggan slide. They have no infallible authority, and without it they are rushing pell-mell to chaos, to tribulation, and to God's judgment on a society that has supplanted His Word with human opinion.

—*William MacDonald, November-December 1993, pp. 6-7*

64. THE VISION

issionaries seem to be looked upon as those who are "indulging in fanciful theories" or are "impractical," as the Oxford English Dictionary describes them. Yet how much we owe to men of true vision. Those who can see beyond the present cloying circumstance and penetrate the mists of uncertain goals, who rally the young, awaken the sleeping, stir up the old as to what might yet be accomplished for God in whatever time is left.

It is men of vision that shake the cobwebs from barren religious forms, get out of their comfortable pews and the security of the status quo, and face the cold blast of reality, where lost sinners die with broken hearts and broken lives, crying out, *"I looked on my right hand, and beheld, but there was no man that would know me: refuge failed me; no man cared for my soul"* (Ps. 142:4).

Preaching in a gospel meeting some years ago, on the prodigal son, I went through Luke 15, point by point, and at last got the prodigal coming back to his father, where there was bread enough and to spare. It was pointed out that the young man made some serious mistakes, and one of them was that he mistook the father's heart. For when he was still a great way off, his father saw him, and *"ran and fell on his neck, and kissed him."* Then I added with feeling, "He covered him with kisses—pig-smelling rags and all." A call was given to "come home," an appropriate hymn was sung, the meeting ended.

Greeting people at the door, suddenly I was confronted with a poor specimen of a man, introduced by a friend who had brought him in to hear the gospel. "He wants to be saved," said the friend. Well, he looked like a prodigal, unwashed, unshaven. He was, I learned, alcoholic and seriously addicted to drugs, the effects of which had wrought havoc on his body and he smelled heavily.

We sat down together and went over the Scriptures slowly and carefully, trying to make sure this poor fellow understood what was involved. At last he said, "I want to be saved—now." I pointed out that now he must tell the Lord what was on his heart in all honesty.

I had a wee pray and told the Lord he was coming to talk with Him. He started to pray—stumbling, fumbling for words, but they were words of sincerity and honesty as he told the Lord the depths of his sin. As he went on, he bent lower and lower, until he slipped off the bench onto his knees, lower still, on to both hands and knees, his head touching the floor, tears flowing—his and mine. I kneeled beside him. He called on the Lord to save him. Then he rose to his feet, turned to us, and said simply and with conviction, "Now, I am saved!"

The friend who had brought him, herself saved from an unsavory life on the street—now a shining evidence of the grace of God—threw her arms around him with tears of joy. All I could hear was the echo of my own words, "covered him with kisses—pig-smelling rags and all." All right, Mr. Preacher with your 5-point sermon, what about it?

Well, the Lord helped the poor preacher, and he too threw his arms around the new-born man and rejoiced at the wondrous love and grace of the One who could eat with publicans and sinners, touch the leper, and love us to death, even death on a cross.

Trouble is, I think some of us prefer our prodigals already showered, shaved, and fragrant. Are we really spiritually prepared for the results of a *"whosoever"* gospel? Do we need a true vision of the lost, the Saviour's vision, that overflowed in tears? Do we see the lost in their hopelessness and danger of eternal perdition. That is, eternal—forever and forever. We call them "unsaved"—a more comfortable word than the one the Lord used—"lost"! *"Where there is no vision, the people perish"* (Prov. 29:18).

Yet there is a word of warning for our days. We must be careful about claims of "vision." Indeed those who would claim to have "vision" must be carefully examined. We read of some who *"err in vision"* and of others who *"speak a vision of their own heart and not out of the mouth of the Lord."*

The test of true vision is, of course, the Word of God. The Lord will not give a vision of any thing or work that contravenes the Scriptures and goes against divine principles. These are not negotiable.

What is needed first is a fresh vision of the Lord Jesus before the soul. This is not the result of dreamy religious thoughts, but by the diligent exercise of faith, beholding Christ in the mirror of the Word (2 Cor. 3:18). Peter reminds us that diligently adding in our faith the Christian virtues will ensure fruitfulness in the knowledge of the Lord Jesus. Thus, he says, we will not be lacking in either clear vision or sharp focus (2 Pet. 1:5-9).

Turn your eyes upon Jesus,
Look full in His wonderful face,
And the things of earth will grow strangely dim,
In the light of His glory and grace.
(Helen H. Lemmel)

—*J. Boyd Nicholson, Editorial, March-April 1998, p. 3*

65. HE PUT AWAY SIN (HEB. 9:26)

 ne of the incomprehensible wonders of the Lord Jesus Christ, our Saviour, relates to sin, and the work He has done in putting it away. We read in 1 Peter 2:22, *"He did no sin."* In other words, our Lord Jesus Christ absolutely never sinned. Nor, in fact, could He ever sin.

Peter goes on to say that this sinless One committed Himself to the Father *"who judgeth righteously."* Does it not follow, in logical terms, that it would be rank injustice to cause One who had never sinned to suffer for the sins that had been committed by others? Yet, the reality is, as Peter further records, that this impeccable One *"...His own self bare our sins in His own body on the tree"* (1 Pet. 2:24). Our Saviour, at Calvary, did not hide Himself from the righteous judgment His creatures' sin deserved.

Paul adds to this theme as he tells us that, *"Him who knew no sin He made to be sin on our behalf"* (2 Cor. 5:21, RV). In other words, though it is beyond our comprehension, the One who knew no sin whatsoever in any personal sense, actually came to be divinely identified with our sin as our substitute sacrifice. This miracle of identification with sin, on the part of the perfectly righteous One, had an absolutely just purpose: *"that we might be made the righteousness of God in Him."*

So it is that God, acting in justice, made His perfect Son to be so identified with our sin that we might become eternal examples of God's perfect righteousness. For, inasmuch as our sin being *"laid upon Him"* came to be as if it were His own, we who are *"saved through faith,"* who are the benefactors of His amazing love and His perfect sacrifice, are made as if we had never sinned at all!

And yet, in all of this amazing work that put away sin eternally, the Sin-bearer never became a sinner! He became the substitute for the sinner. Not in an act that was simply misguided vengeance, but rather, He, united with the Father, engaged in a work that accepted on Himself the full burden of man's sin at Calvary. And then, so great, so perfect, so infinite, so absolute was that holy work of sin-bearing that He—the perfect sacrifice—actually put sin away. He purged it! He removed it utterly!

Alas, there are those who cling to their sin, those who find more pleasure in their sins than they find in the Saviour who died at Calvary for them. They will never enjoy the benefits of that perfect sacrifice achieved at Calvary. These shall go away into everlasting punishment (Mt. 25:46). Upon these, because of their rejection of Christ, will lie forever the stigma of their sin. The sin they chose to love, the iniquity they multiplied, until at last they sealed it with the ultimate sin of rejecting the Saviour, will plunge them down to deepest darkness and eternal suffering. These will be shut outside God's heaven, removed from God's loving memory, and their names blotted out of the Book of Life. Beyond hope, beyond recovery. Put away in their sin, abandoned by the God who would have saved them.

The redeemed soul joins with the lover in Solomon's Song 4:7 to exclaim: *"Thou art all fair, my love; there is no spot in thee."* Yes, He is spotless and undefiled, having restored that which He took not away. The impeccable Christ, who bore our sins and who was made sin for us, now sits enthroned above the heavens. He is in the holiest of all places. His presence there assures us that He was indeed, in those dark hours on the cross, identified with our sin, and that He did put sin away. It can never touch Him again. Its dark clouds can never come rolling back to enshroud His throne. He sits there, in glory, accepted of God, having made one sacrifice for sins forever.

—Doug Kazen, January-February 1997, p. 14

66. The Tenderness of God

hen we think on God, His might and His majesty, His infinite and superlative glories and the blazing radiance of His presence, it seems difficult to reconcile such expansive thoughts with the *tenderness* of God. Yet time and again we read some of the most touching evidences of this aspect of His character.

The opening verses of our Bible describe the creation of heaven and earth. We cannot even begin to imagine what vast explosions of power, what blazing outpourings of energy, what burstings forth of worlds without number in fiery birth accompanied that mighty work, *ex nihilo*—out of nothing, But when God focused His activity on the tiny planet He would prepare as a paradise for His creature, man, all was quiet: *"The Spirit of God moved [gently] upon the face of the waters."*

The special participle, translated *"moved"* occurs only twice in the Old Testament. The other occasion is in Deuteronomy 32:11, describing the Lord's care of His people, Israel, as a mother eagle that *"fluttereth [hovers] over her young."* What tenderness is implicit in this word.

When Adam's form lay immobile in the dust, we might expect that a thundering fiat from God would command His noblest handiwork to rise to life and light and love. But no such sound is heard. It was the tender breathing of the Almighty that gently awakened this first human soul to life.

How many times did the Psalmist rejoice that the *"tender mercies"* of the Lord are over all His works.

How beautifully the Lord Jesus expresses the tenderness of God's heart. He was tender with the little children, with the repentant, the sorrowing, and with the weary multitude, seeing them as sheep having no shepherd.

He could have healed the leper from across the street, or across the city, but with tenderness *"He touched him,"* for He knew how long it had been since he had felt the touch of a loving hand.

How tender He is in dealing with the fainting servant and the bruised instrument. When the flickering flame is almost out and no music comes from the heart, He tenderly moves to fan the flame and raise the song again.

No wonder Isaiah takes this up as a theme in the first of the Servant Songs in his book: *"A bruised reed shall He not break, and the smoking flax shall He not quench"* (Isa. 42:3). After the home-call of a renowned servant of the Lord, many years ago, the following lines were found written in the flyleaf of his old Bible:

The reed was bruised, no music sweet
Could from the lute the player make,
It seemed as if it were more meet
To break it and another make.

But One in pity saw the bruise,
And smoothed it out and made it straight,
Fit for Himself again to use,
Of His grand harmony partake.

O God, I am that bruiséd reed,
My songs of grace must almost cease;
Refit me for Thy service need,
Bring from me hymns of joy and peace.

The oil was spent within the lamp,
The flickering wick, tho' still alight,
With moistened oil was scarcely damp,
And every moment grew less bright.

But One stood by and saw the spark,
Who would not quench it, but He came,
Lest it should fade into the dark,
He poured in oil, renewed the flame.

O God, I am that smoking flax,
My feeble flame is burning low;

Breathe on me, Spirit of the Lord,
And cause the light once more to glow.

He led me by the way of pain,
A barren and a starless place;
(I didn't know His eyes were wet),
He would not let me see His face.

He left me like a frightened child,
Unshielded in a night of storm,
(How should I dream He was so near?)
The rain-swept darkness hid His form.

But when the clouds were driven back,
And dawn was breaking into day,
I knew whose feet had walked with mine,
I saw His footprints all the way.
                    (George Goodman)

How grateful we are for all His tender dealings with us, and His longsuffering patience towards us. We can affirm with James, *"The Lord is very pitiful, and of tender mercy"* (Jas. 5:11).

—*J. Boyd Nicholson, Editorial, May-June 1997, p. 3*

67. THE GOLDEN YEARS

rom the context of John 21:18-23, we gather that Peter was a middle-aged man. The Lord spoke to him about a time *"when thou wast young"* (past tense) and then *"when thou shalt be old"* (future tense). He was neither young nor old, so we may conclude that he was middle-aged. However, it was at this stage of his life that the Lord gave him some details concerning the manner in which he would end his earthly life, in order that he might direct the remaining years accordingly.

MID-LIFE CRISIS

In the world we hear much about the "mid-life crisis" that strikes so many as they begin to realize that the most of life is behind them, and they are now on the "home stretch" as it were. Indeed, middle-age is a time to undertake a serious evaluation of the purpose and direction of our lives, and to ensure that we are living for eternity. Peter is unique in that he alone of all the disciples was given a glimpse into what the future held for him as he would near the end of life.

"When thou wast young...when thou shalt be old" (v. 18). These statements bracket the entire life span of every human being. The Lord reminds Peter of what it was like to be young: *"Thou girdest thyself, and walkedst whither thou wouldest."* Then he reminds him of what it will be like to be old: *"Another shall gird thee, and carry thee whither thou wouldest not."*

YOUTH AND OLD AGE

The marks of youth are independence and freedom. It is time when we can take charge, and do whatever we want. The marks of age are those of dependence and limitation, a time when the increasing restrictions of age bring us to a position where others are required to do things for us and make decisions on our behalf. Not all of these are necessarily what we ourselves would choose: *"whither thou wouldest not."* As far as Peter was concerned, the Lord said this to signify *"by what death he should glorify God"* (v. 19).

In man's world, death is viewed as the final indignity, but not so in God's terms. In this statement we learn how that even death can be *"for the glory of God."* We see this in the death of Lazarus. When the Lord heard that Lazarus was sick He said to the disciples, *"This sickness is not unto death, but for the glory of God."* It would have been comparatively easy for the Lord to have intervened then and to have kept Lazarus from dying, but the Lord had greater things in mind. Lazarus would not be delivered from dying, but from death itself, thus bringing a greater glory to God.

We see this also in the attitude of Paul towards his own death as he wrote, *"...so now also Christ shall be magnified in my body, whether it be by life or by death."* Paul saw that death could be an opportunity to *"magnify Christ."* Again, as we noted in a previous article, the apostle spoke of his impending death as a final act of sacrifice, the worshipful drink offering poured out on his years of service, thus bringing glory to God.

DEATH AND GLORY

The deaths of the martyrs, from Stephen onwards, most surely have brought glory to God, and we can all recount how God was glorified in the passing of many we have known during our own lifetime as they faced death with confidence, courage, and submission to His will.

Much is said in our ministry as to how we should live, but naturally, we do not easily speak about how we might die, and yet Scripture is not silent on this important subject. The fact is that death is something we need to hear more about and how we can face it for the glory of God.

"FOLLOW ME"

After the Lord had revealed to Peter the manner by which he would glorify God in his death, He gave him a fresh commission as

He said, *"Follow Me."* Even later, when Peter with his natural impetuous curiosity asked the Lord about John's future, the Lord simply said, *"What is that to thee? Follow thou Me."* Peter first heard that same call when as a young man he worked at the fishing trade with his father. He heard the Lord say then, *"Follow Me,"* and he had obeyed. Now, some years later, he hears the call renewed, *"Follow thou Me."*

A RENEWED COMMISSION

Many of us look back to a time in our youth when we were saved, when we heard His voice calling us to the path of obedience and service, and we followed Him. But time and circumstance take their toll and by the time middle-age arrives, perhaps it is time for us to hear the call afresh, *"Follow Me."* It is time to put behind us all the things that have discouraged us in our circumstances and in ourselves. It is time, like Peter, to put the failures behind us, and to *"follow"* again with renewed vigor and commitment. Peter did that and the Lord mightily used him to be the apostle who led the great work of world evangelism and the opening of the door to the Gentiles shortly thereafter. All this began with him hearing afresh the call of his Lord, saying, *"Follow thou Me."*

"TILL I COME"

Peter was curious about the future of John and the Lord refused to reveal that to him, save only to say, *"If I will that he tarry till I come, what is that to thee?"* The truth of the return of the Lord for his own was not fully revealed until Paul wrote about it to the Corinthians and to the Thessalonians. But here the Lord opens up the possibility that some might remain until He comes again, while others will be called to pass through death. What a blessed hope this is for believers today! Whether we live or die, we are the Lord's, and as we look at the rapidly deteriorating conditions in the world today, we feel that the coming of the Lord for His Church must be very close indeed.

It is possible that there are many living today who will never know what it is to die. They will be changed and raptured, caught up with loved ones gone before to meet Him in the air, and *"so shall we ever be with the Lord."* From the depths of our hearts we can say with John, *"Even so, come, Lord Jesus."*

> *O joy, O delight, should we go without dying,*
> *No sickness, no sadness, no dread and no crying,*
> *Caught up through the clouds with our Lord into glory,*
> *When Jesus receives His own.* (H. L. Turner)

—W. H. Burnett, July-August 1996, pp. 4-5

68. BILL JUST WOULDN'T FORGET

e was a stubborn old Scot, was Bill. The elders warned us about him. He only came out to hear the gospel if the preacher had the same dialect as he. He figured another Scot wouldn't do him any harm. Well, he got a double dose one night, for there were two preachers and both of them had that particular twist to their tongues; both were from his homeland.

He had been in the fellowship of that local church forty years before. Then there was some trouble and Bill left in anger. His wife, a wee gentle soul, would not "forsake the gathering" and she maintained her fellowship with the believers. Bill would drive her to the door. She went in alone and he would go home. Then he'd return after the meeting to pick her up. He did that for forty long years.

The warning the elders gave us was, "Don't buttonhole Bill at the door." He had a short fuse. We were just to greet him and be thankful he had come out. The few times he attended we were careful, especially for his gentle wife's sake.

One time, however, it was different. He and his wife came in and sat towards the front. That meeting was directed by the Spirit to behold most tenderly the cross and the suffering Saviour. The Lord touched hearts and there were tears.

We stood at the door greeting the people as they left. Then along came Bill. His head was down, and as I greeted him, he looked up. His eyes were brimming and his checks were wet. My heart went out to him. I could not restrain myself as I thought of all he was missing. I put my arm around his shoulder, "Oh, Bill," I said, "I wish you were in fellowship with your brethren."

"I wish I was," he replied.

"Do you mean that, Bill?"

"With all my heart."

"We'll be up to see you in the morning." So he left.

Next morning after breakfast, we went to his home. He welcomed us and led us out to a little summer house in the back garden. There

227

he poured out a sad story of trouble with his brethren. Forty years had passed and he was still angry at those men—and they were all dead but Bill!

We asked him if he would meet with the elders. Yes, he would. That evening we met in a little room, Bill, the elders, and the two of us, just as his friends.

One brother said, "We'd better pray first" and so round the circle, one after the other, we stood to pray for Bill and the problem. Then it was Bill's turn. Would he pray? Suddenly, Bill got to his feet and in a flood of tears poured out his heart to the Lord. That was the meeting! The brethren rose and threw their arms around him— reconciled. Then Bill said, "Brethren, I've lost forty years of my life for God because I would neither forget nor forgive."

There are some things it is important to remember. It is good to remember *"the former days"* when we first became *"companions"* of the believers in Christ (Heb. 11:32). David encouraged himself in a day of distress when he recalled good times in the past with God in the sanctuary (Ps. 63:2). He rejoiced in the night at the remembrance of the Lord's protection and sustaining hand (Ps. 63:6-7).

Paul, however, assures us there are some things good to forget.

The things that should have been: the disappointments of life, especially associated with the service of others towards us. The remembrance of these failed expectations only breed bitterness and blame. That was Bill's problem. He felt others had failed him and he was not going to forget. So he lost forty years of fellowship.

Paul recognized that the Philippians had lacked in their service towards him (2:30). But long ago he had put the sorrow of it out of his mind and he thanked God for every remembrance of them (1:3).

The things that might have been: the frustrations of life, associated with personal ambitions. The remembrance of these only breed discouragement and despair. Paul counted those things but rubbish (3:8). How many waste the present moment lamenting over lost opportunities: "If only…"

The things that cannot be: the impossibilities of life, because of having yielded all to Christ. The remembrance of these only rob us of present opportunities. We must quit knocking on doors the Lord has closed. Forget it! Paul did—and gained Christ.

Well, Bill is in the glory now, but he lived a few years to prove that the work of grace in his heart was real. We'll never forget that first Lord's day after his reconciliation. He pulled up as usual to the door and let his wife out. Then he parked the car! Together they walked in and took their seat among the believers. We all dissolved in thankfulness.

What marvellous grace that God is able to say, because of Calvary, *"And their sins and iniquities will I remember no more"* (Heb. 10:17). May we all have grace to forget what we should forget and remember what we should remember.

—J. Boyd Nicholson, Editorial, July-August 2000, p. 3

69. IN A PLACE WHERE TWO WAYS MET (JN. 12:12-28)

hen Israel's true King, the Lord Jesus, entered triumphantly into Jerusalem five days before the Passover of His crucifixion, the extent of the glory given to Him was the insincere Hosannas of the people and a place on the back of a donkey's colt. Zechariah the prophet had predicted it perfectly with rebuke: *"Rejoice greatly, O daughter of Zion; shout, O daughter of Jerusalem; behold thy King cometh unto thee: He is just, and having salvation; lowly and riding upon an ass, and upon a colt, the foal of an ass."*

How fittingly had God arranged this scene. In Mark's Gospel alone we are told that the two disciples who brought the colt to the Saviour found that donkey *"in a place where two ways met."* This tribute to the glory of the King of kings was found where the two ways met. What were the two ways where this token of His kingly arrival was waiting?

When John describes the same day, he tells us that the disciples would not understand this triumphal entry into Jerusalem until Jesus was glorified. On that day, two ways met in the Saviour. Greeks from the west came who said, *"Sirs, we would see Jesus."* But this way, out from the wisdom of Greece, crossed another ancient path that day. They came in the hour of His death, to cross paths with those who had come thirty-three years before from the east. The wise men, the star-gazers, who had followed His star, had come to Him, not at His hour of death, but at the hour of His birth. Their inquiry was, *"Where is He that is born king of the Jews? For we have seen His star in the east, and are come to worship Him."*

The key to seeing Him then was glory. Herod never saw this. That was revealed to poor, lowly shepherds: *"Glory to God in the highest and on earth peace, good will toward men"*—and they returned glorifying and praising God. When those two ways met in Him, the wisdom of the east and of the west, the key to seeing Him was still glory: the glory of the Christ in the meeting of the path to His birth and the path to His death.

The Saviour's answer to Andrew and Philip who relayed the request of the Greeks to see Him, was astounding. *"The hour is come, that the Son of man should be glorified. Verily, verily, I say unto you, Except a corn of wheat fall into the ground and die, it abideth alone: but if it die, it bringeth forth much fruit."* This corn of wheat, living on the stalk, has a glory all its own while it waves in the breeze, golden as the sunshine that bathes it. But it must fall into the ground and die to bear fruit. Its glory will be greater if it dies.

The Lord Jesus came into the world, was crucified, raised and glorified to bring many sons to glory. Two ways met that day, and they tell us that wisdom will only truly see Jesus when it sees the glory of His life: it was unto death, in view of a great harvest.

In that glorious life and death two ways met. The pathway of the Son of God coming forth from the Father into the world, and the pathway of the Son of God leaving the world and returning to the Father met at the cross. The ways of mercy and truth were met together in that death, and in that death righteousness and peace kissed each other, as the righteous One made peace through the blood of His cross. Truth sprung out of the earth as the Lord Jesus in His incarnation became a real man. Truth was there displayed as He became a sacrifice for sin. The corn of wheat that fell, died. Righteousness looked down from heaven to meet truth, as the Father continually sent forth His approval—and on more than one occasion audibly—of His Son in whom He was well pleased. In death much fruit; in resurrection much glory.

The daughters of Zion missed the glory and the rejoicing that day, the glory of a lovely life lived and the sacrificial death He would die. Their empty "Hosannas" caused the Lord Jesus to weep over Jerusalem. But God was watching over the glory of His Son and when the Son prayed, *"Father, glorify Thy name,"* the answer was, *"I have both glorified it, and will glorify it again."* In spite of everything, there would always be those who would seek to know the glory of His death—even if it was not when they untied a colt outside the door in a place where two ways met. Let us make His praise glorious in the remembrance of that life unto death.

—David B. Robins, May-June 1996, p. 11

70. Harvest Past, Summer Ended

What a beautiful time of the year! The sumac blazing red on the hills, maples glorious in their scarlet apparel, the corn and the vine full and fragrant. But how brief it is. Too soon the wind and rains come to strip away the leaves, and we realize how quickly time flies and the summer is ended.

So it was long ago in the days of the weeping prophet, Jeremiah. He profoundly felt the need of the people, the urgency of the day, and the blast of the approaching winter storm that would so soon envelop his people: *"Oh that my head were waters, and mine eyes a fountain of tears."* Why was he so distressed?

Jeremiah had seen a brief summertime of recovery of the people of Judah in the days of Josiah, the good young king, *"that turned to the Lord with all his heart, and with all his soul, and with all his might."* The idols were smashed, their altars destroyed, and the wicked priests put to death. The long-forgotten Passover was restored, and there was none like it since the days of the Judges.

With the tragic death of King Josiah on the battlefield at the age of thirty-nine, the summertime ended for Judah and there was a gradual decay of spiritual, moral, and social conditions. Great nations were struggling for the balance of power and the storm-clouds were gathering. Soon the mighty armies of Nebuchadnezzar would destroy the temple and carry the people away captive to Babylon.

The daughters of Jerusalem raised their voices in sad lament, *"The harvest is past, the summer is ended, and we are not saved."* No wonder Jeremiah wept for the people. They had had no sense of the time of their opportunity. Even the birds, said the Lord, know their times. But they didn't. Now it was too late.

While this scripture has a prophetic application to the nation of Israel, we cannot help but see some striking similarities to the days in which we live. The western world with its religious handmaiden, Christendom, has been the recipient of the bounty of God. A summertime of plenty has blessed these lands on every hand. They have built bigger barns wherewith to store their goods. Their philosophy is, *"Thou hast much goods laid up for many years; take thine ease, eat, drink, and be merry,"* and God is not recognized as the Benefactor of every good and pleasant gift they enjoy.

The great power blocs of the world are rapidly changing. The European Community is rising in power and influence, China is shaking itself, India—second only to China in population—is moving onto the scene, and the African nations are in turmoil. Third World countries now have nuclear capability. Leaders of nations are being deposed for moral, fiscal, and political reasons.

The birds fly south because they know *"their appointed times"* and the summer is ended, but man does not recognize God's call to consider his latter end; nor has he learned that all the goodness of God he enjoys is intended to lead him to repentance.

For the opulent west, their summer is ending. Already we can see the rapid decay in high places; major currencies both east and west are tumbling. Values are perverted. Vehicles worth billions travel in space and the homeless, bereft, die in the streets.

However, there may be a greater crisis coming for this earth. The Lord may come back for His Church. Think of it! On top of all the problems facing this world, suddenly millions will disappear in a moment from every country.

The Church gone! Its influence against the darkness and the corruption of this world gone! Then will fall upon this planet such judgments as have never been known before: the earth, the sea, the sun, moon and stars will all be smitten. So unspeakable will be those terrors that a flying angel will cry, *"Woe, woe, woe, to the inhabiters of the earth..."*

The summer of God's grace will be ended, the harvest of precious souls who put their faith in Christ and His finished work at Calvary, will have been gathered in. Then the mournful refrain of the lost will be *"we are not saved."* Lost forever and forever!

Dear reader, if you are not saved, your summer is ending. Soon it will be too late. Hear the call of the Saviour now, *"He that heareth My word, and believeth on Him that sent Me, hath everlasting life, and shall not come into* [judgment]*; but is passed from death unto life"* (Jn. 5:24). *"Behold, now is the day of salvation"* (2 Cor. 6:2).

233

Dear believer, does it really grip us, that men and women all around us are *lost* and are *now* perishing? Jeremiah wept fountains of tears. When last did I drop one honest tear for perishing souls? Do we care?

> *How oft of thy danger, and guilt He hath told thee!*
> *How oft still the message of mercy doth send!*
> *Haste, haste, while He waits in His arms to enfold thee!*
> *"The harvest is passing, the summer will end."*

—*J. Boyd Nicholson, Editorial, September-October 1998, p. 3*

71. MERCY OR SACRIFICE (HOS. 6:6)

 uring His life on earth our Lord Jesus Christ twice applied a most important precept, *"I will have mercy and not sacrifice"* (Mt. 9:13; 12:7). He quoted from Hosea 6:6, where the prophet described the sin of Ephraim in particular and of Israel in general. When the Lord was criticized on these occasions for violating standards based on human legalism, He stated this divine principle and practice. Worthy sacrifices are always acceptable.

REPENTANCE OR JUDGMENT

There is no sympathy in Scripture for flagrant violation of divine requirements. The entire prophecy of Hosea, while promising blessing upon repentance, makes it clear that the alternative was judgment. However, judgment is God's strange work (Isa. 28:21; 2 Pet. 3:9). Because the Pharisees were self-righteous, they were incapable of going beyond a rigid observance of the law, a law which they had modified by their own human traditions and rituals.

Theirs was a class system in which they placed themselves at the top. But they stood self-condemned. As Jews, they were the objects of divine compassion, yet they failed to recognize either the need of mercy, or their duty to show it to others.

JUDGEMENT TEMPERED WITH MERCY

Divine judgment is always tempered with mercy. While the Lord Jesus never condoned sin, He recognized the need of the fallen, and was ready to meet that need. He denounced the hypocrites and self-righteous more than the base outcasts of society who made no pretense at holiness. He exposed self-vindication, but extended mercy to those who acknowledged their unworthiness.

A striking case in point is the adulterous woman of John 8. With a single question and two terse statements, the Lord both convicted her haughty accusers and mercifully dismissed the guilty sinner. Would either ever forget?

When we realize how merciful God has been to us, we will avoid the self-satisfied ignorance displayed by the church at Laodicea (Rev. 3:17). Paul paused during his description of the spiritual blessings of the Ephesians to remind them of what they were before conversion and their obligation to God's mercy. *"But God, who is rich in mercy, for His great love, wherewith He loved us..."* (Eph. 2:4).

JUSTICE AND MERCY BLENDED

Only a thankless saint fails to recognize his eternal indebtedness to infinite mercy. Micah 6:8 expresses the blending of godly consistency and practical mercy: *"What doth the Lord require of thee, but to do justly, and to love mercy, and to walk humbly with thy God?"* Justice should never be enforced at the expense of mercy. Neither does mercy violate or disregard the claims of justice. When justice and mercy are blended, both are adorned. When justice is set aside for leniency, or mercy is replaced by insensitivity, both become abhorrent. The perfect blend is assured by a humble walk before the Lord.

In such holy fellowship we learn the heart of God and demonstrate it by our treatment of others. The perfect balance of grace and truth is exhibited by the Lord Jesus (Jn. 1:14). With Him, truth was neither eroded by grace nor applied at the expense of grace. The Lord denounced pharisaical hypocrisy and legalism in Matthew 23:23.

LEGALISM OR LICENSE

The combined characteristics of justice, mercy, and faith express the intent of the law. A balance of these is not typical of society today, influenced as it is by human reasoning and restrictions. These virtues flow from a heart touched by divine love and affected by an appreciation of infinite mercy.

The carnal saint cannot comprehend these blended virtues and typically resorts to either legalism or license. Thus both he and the people of God affected by him are brought into unscriptural bondage or unspiritual compromise.

Mercy distinguishes the judgment of sin and the need of the sinner. It judges the fact and gives the benefit of doubt as to the motive. It declares itself regarding the principle and condemns the practice. It separates from all involvement with sin (2 Cor. 6:17), yet does its best to win the sinner. Such distinctions require a wisdom that is *"full of mercy"* and which comes only from above (Jas. 3:17).

—Gary W. Seale, January-February 2000, p. 8

72. THE WINDING SHEET OF TIME

aul gives instructions in 1 Corinthians 7 to the saints at Corinth in regard to marriage relationships, and he uses the expression, *"The time is short."* The word he employs for *"short"* (*sunestalomenos*) occurs only twice in the New Testament—here and in Acts 5:6. There it is used for the wrapping up of the dead body of Ananias in its last winding sheet. The word is derived from the verb, *sustello*, to place together, to draw together, or contract. Vincent says that it is also used for furling a sail or packing up luggage. Paul pictures the foreshortening of the time which must elapse before the coming of the Lord.

The idea is that the period has been so shortened that the Christians should hold earthly ties and relationships loosely.

Just as Ananias was dead and wound up in his winding sheet, so with the present dispensation. Its sails have been furled, its luggage packed; the graveclothes are wrapping it around, and soon it will terminate in the coming of the Lord.

Paul applied this fact to five phases of the Christian's life: marriage, sorrow, joy, commerce, and daily life in the world (1 Cor. 7:29-31). Any of these things are liable to occupy time and attention unduly. All should be viewed from the standpoint of the approaching end of the age. If this was true in Paul's day, how much more so in ours upon whom the end of the age is come.

MARRIAGE

In a heathen community like Corinth there must have been many complicated and difficult cases to settle among the believers. Paul gives a fourfold answer to their questions, summarized at the end by the three principles of verse 39: marriage is for life; marriage must be in the Lord; and marriage must be subordinated to the fact of the imminent return of the Lord. All are not called to completely sever home responsibilities like Paul. On the other hand, some people can make a god of their home and their own comfort.

SORROW

"They that weep as though they wept not" (v. 30). This points to the tragedies and bereavements of life. What tears are shed in secret! It is possible to allow our sorrows to so occupy our thoughts that we have no time for the service of the Lord. Often God's choicest saints are those who drink most deeply of this cup. We must not allow the cares of this life to choke the good seed. Weeping may come in to lodge at eventide but joy comes in the morning.

JOY

Life is not all sorrow and weeping. At times the sun will shine brightly and prosperity will knock at the door. The Christian life is a life of joy but the pleasures and joys of this life are transient. Preoccupation with even our blessings can blind us to the fact that "Men die in darkness at our side, without a hope to cheer the gloom." We are here for such a little while to help pluck them from the burnings.

COMMERCE

"They that buy as though they possessed not" (v. 30). This points to the subtle snare of making money and possessing things. Millionaires have come to be very ordinary individuals. For the Christian now, the piling up of things will be to leave it all behind for the Antichrist and his servants. Scripture exhorts us not be slothful in business, but it is possible to be so occupied with it that we have no time for the things of the Lord.

THE WORLD

"They that use this world as not abusing it." The Christian has been taken out of the world by the cross of Christ, and then sent back into it as an alien (Jn. 17:6, 11). His citizenship and politics are in heaven (Phil. 3:20). Contacts in school, business, and factory are unavoidable and legitimate, but he must never contract an unequal

yoke to become like Lot in Sodom, sitting in the gate and administrating their civic affairs. That would be becoming like one of them.

Thus Paul, in a few brief words, applies the great truth of the shortness of time and the imminence of the coming of our Lord Jesus to our matrimonial, emotional, commercial, and social lives.

—T. Ernest Wilson, January-February 2000, p. 9

73. GOD'S STRATEGY OF WEAK WEAPONS

ow remarkable that God has a deliberate strategy of using *"the weak things of the world to confound the things which are mighty."* Immediately David and the giant of Gath come to mind. There Goliath stood, more than nine feet tall, armed from head to foot with about 150 pounds of brass. His armor alone was likely close to David's full weight!

Saul could not conceive of this stripling going into battle unarmed, and since Israel's hope lay in the outcome, he felt that this shepherd youth should wear the best protection, his very own armor, complete with helmet and sword.

Was size the problem? Remember, Saul was head and shoulders above the people. But the scripture does not say that: *"I cannot go with these; for I have not proved them,"* said David. Surely those professional soldiers would not outfit David in armor ten sizes too big.

David's own armor, however, exactly fitted the need. It bore no burden upon him and it had been already proven with a lion and a bear. He wrote about this protective panoply in Psalm 91, *"The Lord, He is my refuge and my fortress...His truth shall be thy shield and buckler."*

So in the Name of the Lord of hosts, he ran towards the enemy with his sling, and a smooth stone which he propelled as an exclamation mark to his battle cry, right into the forebrain of the giant.

Weak weapons they were! A shepherd's kit against the hordes of Philistia? Well, that is how it appeared, but impelling and directing that one smooth stone was David's God in whom he trusted and for whose holy Name he was jealous.

There is much more than an arrogant giant and a slung stone here. There was the whole issue of the honor of the Name of the Lord. It wasn't the army of Saul, or of Israel, it was *"the armies of the living God."* So God defended His armies that day, and the honor of His Name, with a sling, a stone, and a young shepherd who would trust Him and lay his life on the line as an evidence of his faith.

Then there was that tent peg in the hand of a very brave woman.

Hardly a fearsome weapon. But by it she fastened the glory of the captain of the hosts of Canaan to the ground and *"God subdued on that day Jabin the king of Canaan."*

And what about the host of the Midianites *"as grasshoppers for multitude"*? Among this host was an infantry division of 135,000 swordsmen. Gideon's meager and fearful company of 32,000 were hopelessly outnumbered. They were demoralized as well, for when the opportunity was given for the fearful to resign from the army, almost two-thirds went home! That was not a good day for Gideon.

His force was to be depleted further on orders from the Lord. The remainder was given the water test and only 300 passed! The Lord recognized fear in His servant and told him to go against the Midianites that very night. *"But,"* He said, *"If thou fear..."* Of course he was afraid. Especially when he considered their weaponry: pitchers and lamps in their left hands and trumpets in their right hands. Quite a balancing feat but hardly intimidating.

God, however, was again using His strategy of weak weapons so that the glory of conquest would not go to man, but would be His alone. The pitchers are broken, the trumpets are blown, and the shout is given, *"The sword of the Lord and of Gideon,"* and the enemy in fright and confusion slaughters itself.

What shall we say of a rejected King whose visible army was one fisherman with a sword which he didn't know how to use? *"He was crucified through weakness, yet He liveth by the power of God."*

How often we feel our ineptitude in things eternal and our weakness in the face of the hordes that oppose us. Circumstances may seem to overwhelm us and ride roughshod over our aching hearts, but the Lord is there, standing by in the shadows, waiting to put into effect His strategy of weak weapons, to bring us through to victory in such a way that *"He shall bear the glory!"*

> *I know not what the future hath*
> *Of marvel or surprise,*
> *Assured alone that life and death,*
> *His mercy underlies.*
> *And if my heart and flesh are weak*
> *To bear the untried pain,*

The bruised reed He will not break,
But strengthen and sustain.
I know not where His islands lift,
Their fronded palms in air,
I only know I cannot drift,
Beyond His love and care.
And Thou, O Lord, by whom are seen,
Thy creatures as they be,
Forgive me if too close I lean
My human heart on Thee.
                              (John Greenleaf Whittier)

—*J. Boyd Nicholson, Editorial, January-February 1995, p. 3*

74. Thou Art With Me

 he title is in the center verse of Psalm 23 and is the central thought of this pearl of Psalms. It stands out in relation to six views of the believer's life.

My Need as a Sinner

"The Lord is my Shepherd; I shall not want." His work on the cross is the pledge of my salvation. Green pastures and still waters speak of rest, security and satisfaction—rest of conscience by the pardon He bestows, rest of heart by the peace which He gives, and rest of assurance as the Spirit witnesses with our spirits that we are the children of God.

My Weakness as a Saint

"He restoreth my soul." His advocacy is the pledge of my restoration. What mistakes we have made in the past! What failures we have been! So many of us have been vessels marred in the hand of the Potter; but let us take courage, *"He restoreth my soul." "He made it again another vessel, as seemed good to the Potter to make it"* (Jer. 18:4), Oh, to be like clay, passive in the hand of the heavenly Potter, responsive to His gentle touch! If we will only let Him, He will fashion us according to His own blessed design.

My Perplexities in the Path

"He leadeth me in the paths of righteousness for His Name's sake." We need the unerring guidance of the Shepherd, and His presence is the pledge of the guidance. The Shepherd goes before the sheep and they follow Him (Jn. 10:4). Some He will lead into private paths of service, others into public paths, but it is always His to lead and ours to follow. In His life down here, He left us a perfect pattern.

In His service He sought all kinds of people in all sorts of places and saturated His whole life's work with prayer. Paul cried, *"That I may know Him, and the power of His resurrection, and the fellowship of His sufferings."*

In John 12 at Bethany we see three lovers of Christ exemplifying this great ambition of the soul. Martha knew Him; Lazarus knew the power of His resurrection, and Mary knew the fellowship of His sufferings. The paths of service into which the Shepherd leads hold trials and difficulties, but His unerring guidance and wisdom is never denied us.

MY SORROWS BY THE WAY

"Yea, though I walk through the valley of the shadow of death...." His priestly sympathy and power are the pledge of my comfort and succor. *"Many are the afflictions of the righteous;"* yet *"In all their affliction He was afflicted"* (Isa. 63:9). Hearts may be torn, crushed and bleeding, and doubts may fill the mind as to why, yet behind the inscrutable wisdom which permitted it all there is the gracious ministry of our Great High Priest.

With what understanding and sympathy does He enter into the sorrows of His own. *"Every branch that beareth fruit, He purgeth it,"* yet never is the Husbandman so near the vine as when He is purging. His loving aim is more fruit: fruit by union, more fruit by purging, much fruit by abiding (Jn. 15). In the dark valley of trial "clouds and darkness round us press." Like the disciples on the Holy Mount, we fear to enter the cloud. Its melancholy gloom frightens us, yet when the cloud is past we saw *"no man save Jesus only."* *"Thou art with me, Thy rod and Thy staff they comfort me."* In the green pastures he talked about the Shepherd, in the valley he talked to Him.

Be still, my soul; thy best, thy Heavenly Friend
Through thorny ways leads to a joyful end.
Be still, my soul; the waves and winds still know
His voice who ruled them while He dwelt below.
Be still, my soul; the Sun of life divine
Through palling clouds shall but more brightly shine. (K.S.)

My Day of Conflict

"Thou preparest a table...in the presence of mine enemies." The power of His might in Ephesians 6:10 is the pledge of my victory. A table spread in the presence of my enemies for divine satisfaction and derived from His fullness is the pilgrim-warrior's portion. Here too, in the field of battle, and not only in the green pastures, we find the anointed head and the overflowing cup, *"for the joy of the Lord is your strength."*

Three times in Romans 8 the gauntlet is thrown down in the face of the enemy: by the Father (v. 33), by the Son (v. 34), and by the Spirit (v. 35)—no accusation, no condemnation, no separation.

Four times in that grand chapter of victory we read *"for us."* The Father is for us in justification (v. 32); the Son is for us in acceptance (v. 34), *"accepted in the Beloved;"* the Spirit is for us in intercession (v. 26). No wonder the chapter closes with the triumphant doxology of the saints: *"Nay, in all these things we are more than conquerors through Him that loved us."*

My Day of Departure

His blessed promise is the assurance that the Father's house becomes the home of the saints. *"I will dwell in the house of the Lord forever."* Here is the end of our pilgrimage. No more wanderings. No more perplexities in our anxiety to discern the mind of the Lord. Our sorrows and trials will all be over, for *"God shall wipe away all tears from their eyes."* Our conflict with the forces of evil will be at an end. The Father's house becomes my heavenly home forever. It is guaranteed by our Saviour's word (Jn. 14:2) and confirmed by His own prayer in John 17:24, *"Father, I will that they also, whom Thou hast given Me, be with Me where I am; that they may behold My glory."* May we live in the light of the cross and the glory *"until the day break, and the shadows flee away."*

—Robert McClurkin, July-August 1996, pp. 10-11

SCRIPTURE INDEX